GUIDE TO

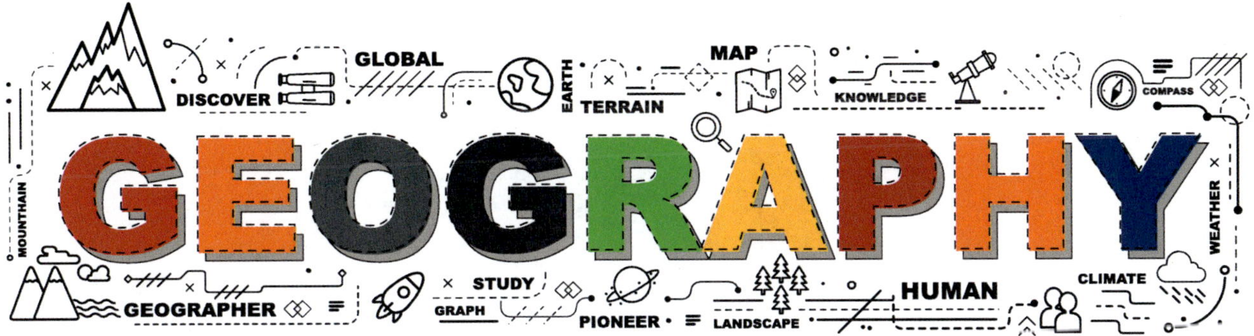

An OMNI LEARNING CENTER Educational Guide

LORRAINE GERSTL

GUIDE TO GEOGRAPHY

An OMNI LEARNING CENTER Educational Guide

ISBN 978-1-950134-36-6
Omni Learning Center Educational Guides
an Imprint of Pangæa Publishing Group

Lorraine Gerstl cover photo by Marc Howard

Pangaea by Kieff, Latitude and Longitude of the Earth by Djexplo,
Spreading homo sapiens by NordNordWest / Public domain
CC BY-SA 3.0 Wikimedia Commons

Cover & interior design and typesetting by
DesignPeaks@gmail.com

The book is available at special quantity discounts for bulk purchase.
For details, write to: *sales@OmniLearningCenter.org*

25579 Carmel Knolls Drive, Carmel - CA, 93923
Telephone: 831-277-3387 / 831-224-0742
contact@OmniLearningCenter.org
www.OmniLearningCenter.org

To

To Greg, Karen, Roslyn, Jeff & Tracy
and to Oliver, Fineas, Vivian, Jake, Abby, and Ryland
who are the geographers of tomorrow,
to Michele Morton for her unflagging friendship and support,

and, of course, and as always

for my Hugo

ACKNOWLEDGMENTS

I gratefully thank and appreciate the editorial support and assistance of Wendy Rosenthal, Liese Murphree, Michele Guido, Leslie Turini-Smith, and the brilliant cover and interior design and final editorial guidance of Lisa Peaks.

TABLE OF CONTENTS

INTRODUCTION 9

PART ONE: PHYSICAL GEOGRAPHY 10

PANGÆA — ONE GIANT CONTINENT 11

WHY IS THE EARTH ROUND?...OR IS IT? 12

TECTONIC PLATES — THE SURFACE OF THE EARTH IS IN CONSTANT MOTION 12

LATITUDE AND LONGITUDE — WHERE IN THE WORLD ARE YOU? 12

LATITUDE — ARE YOU NORTH OR ARE YOU SOUTH? 13

LONGITUDE — ARE YOU EAST OR ARE YOU WEST? 14

FUN FACTS ABOUT THE INTERNATIONAL DATE LINE 15

HOW LATITUDE AND LONGITUDE WORK TOGETHER 16

THE POLES — THE ENDS OF THE EARTH 16

WHAT ARE THE GEOGRAPHIC (TRUE) NORTH AND SOUTH POLES? 16

THE GEOGRAPHIC NORTH POLE 17

FUN FACTS ABOUT THE GEOGRAPHIC NORTH POLE 17

THE GEOGRAPHIC SOUTH POLE 18

FUN FACTS ABOUT THE GEOGRAPHIC SOUTH POLE 18

THE POLES ARE POLAR OPPOSITES IN OTHER WAYS TOO 18

WHAT IS THE MAGNETIC NORTH POLE? 18

WHY DOES THE EARTH HAVE A MAGNETIC FIELD? 19

THE COMPASS — HOW WE GET FROM HERE TO THERE 19

FUN FACTS ABOUT COMPASSES 20

THE EARTH'S HEMISPHERES — IF A HEMISPHERE IS HALF THE EARTH, HOW COME THERE ARE FOUR HEMISPHERES? 20

FUN FACTS ABOUT THE HEMISPHERES 20

WHAT CAUSES THE SEASONS? 21

LONGEST AND SHORTEST DAYS 22

MAPS AND CHARTS — PUTTING PEN TO PAPER AND MAKING SENSE OF IT ALL 23

THE DIFFERENCE BETWEEN A MAP AND A GLOBE 24

FIVE ELEMENTS OF ANY MAP 24

THE WATER CYCLE — WATER, WATER EVERYWHERE 25

EVAPORATION 25

CONDENSATION 25

PRECIPITATION *25*
COLLECTION *26*
EROSION — THE EARTH'S SANDPAPER 27
FUN FACTS ABOUT EROSION *28*
GLACIERS — THE EARTH'S ICY BULLDOZERS 29
FUN FACTS ABOUT GLACIERS *29*
CLIMATE AND WEATHER — CLIMATE IS WHAT WE EXPECT, WEATHER IS WHAT WE GET! 30
WHAT IS CLIMATE CHANGE? 30
GLOBAL WARMING — WHEN EVEN THE SHADOWS NEED SHADOWS TO COOL OFF 31
WHAT'S DIFFERENT ABOUT THE CURRENT GLOBAL WARMING? *32*
WHAT CAN WE DO ABOUT IT? *32*
NATURAL WEATHER PHENOMENA 33
HURRICANES — A LOT OF WIND *33*
FUN FACTS ABOUT HURRICANES *33*
TORNADOES — C'MON, BABY, LET'S DO THE TWIST! *34*
FUN FACTS ABOUT TORNADOES *34*
WHAT IS THE DIFFERENCE BETWEEN A TORNADO AND A HURRICANE? 35
MONSOONS 36
FUN FACTS ABOUT MONSOONS *36*
TSUNAMIS — MORE THAN BIG WAVES 36
FUN FACTS ABOUT TSUNAMIS *37*
EARTHQUAKES — WHOLE LOTTA SHAKIN' GOING ON 37
FUN FACTS ABOUT EARTHQUAKES *39*
VOLCANOES — EARTH'S PRESSURE COOKER 40
FUN FACTS ABOUT VOLCANOES *41*
CONTINENTS — A REALLY "BIG" DEAL 42
FUN FACTS ABOUT THE CONTINENTS *42*
ISLANDS 46
FUN FACTS ABOUT ISLANDS *46*
MOUNTAINS 46
FUN FACTS ABOUT MOUNTAINS *47*
RIVERS — THEY JUST KEEP ROLLING ALONG 47
FUN FACTS ABOUT RIVERS *49*
OCEANS AND SEAS 50
FUN FACTS ABOUT OCEANS AND SEAS *50*
OCEAN CURRENTS — U-HAULS OF THE OCEANS 51
THE GULF STREAM *51*
FUN FACTS ABOUT OCEAN CURRENTS *52*

BIOMES — WHERE IS MY HOME? ... 52
FOREST BIOMES ... 53
WHAT MAKES A FOREST A TEMPERATE FOREST? ... 53
WHAT MAKES A FOREST A TAIGA FOREST? ... 53
WHAT MAKES A FOREST A TROPICAL RAINFOREST? ... 54
FUN FACTS ABOUT TROPICAL RAINFORESTS ... 55
GRASSLAND BIOMES ... 55
TUNDRA BIOME ... 56
FUN FACTS ABOUT THE TUNDRA ... 57
DESERT BIOME ... 57
FUN FACTS ABOUT THE DESERT ... 57
AQUATIC BIOMES ... 58
MARINE BIOME ... 58
FUN FACTS ABOUT MARINE BIOMES ... 59
FRESHWATER BIOME ... 59
WETLANDS — MIGRATION STOP, HOTEL, RESTAURANT, NURSERY ... 60
FUN FACTS ABOUT WETLANDS ... 61

PART TWO: HUMAN GEOGRAPHY ... 62
OUR JOURNEY BEGINS ... 63
THE IN-BETWEEN TIMES ... 64
AGRICULTURE AND DOMESTICATION — THE WORLD TURNED UPSIDE DOWN ... 65
NEW IDEAS, NEW KNOWLEDGE, AND A NEW WAY OF LIFE ... 66
THE RISE OF CITIES, THE RISE OF NATIONS ... 67
CHALLENGES FOR TODAY AND TOMORROW ... 67
AIR POLLUTION ... 67
LAND POLLUTION ... 68
WATER POLLUTION ... 69
NOISE POLLUTION ... 70
SPACE POLLUTION ... 70
FOOD POLLUTION ... 71
PLASTIC POLLUTION — CAN TINY PIECES OF LITTER FORM AN ISLAND? ... 71
FRIGHTENING FACTS ABOUT POLLUTION ... 73

PART THREE: FLEX YOUR GEO-MUSCLES AND BUILD YOUR GEO-SKILLS ... 74-154

INTRODUCTION

If it is about Earth's land, water, air, or living things, especially people, it is geography. **Physical geographers** study landforms, water, soil, climate, and the distribution of living things. **Human geographers** explore ways people interact with the environment.

Geography can be traced back to Eratosthenes, a Greek scholar (276-196 B.C.E.), who estimated the circumference of the Earth with relative accuracy by using the angles of shadows, the distance between two cities, and a mathematical formula. Greco-Roman astronomer, geographer, and mathematician Claudius Ptolemy, who lived in Alexandria, Egypt, in 150 A.D., defined the purpose of geography as providing "a view of the whole Earth by mapping the location of places."

Later, Islamic scholars developed the grid system to make maps more accurate. In China, the magnetic compass (invented for divination) was later used for navigation in 1040. European explorers started using the magnetic compass in the following century.

The word 'geography' originates from two Greek words, "geo," which means the Earth and "graphy," which refers to writing, *ergo*, "writing about the Earth." Geography is the science that deals with the description of the Earth's surface.

Learning geography helps us develop an understanding of the interdependence of our world and how we are connected through location, place, movement, region, history, and culture. This understanding helps build awareness for cultural diversity — how and why people live the way they do.

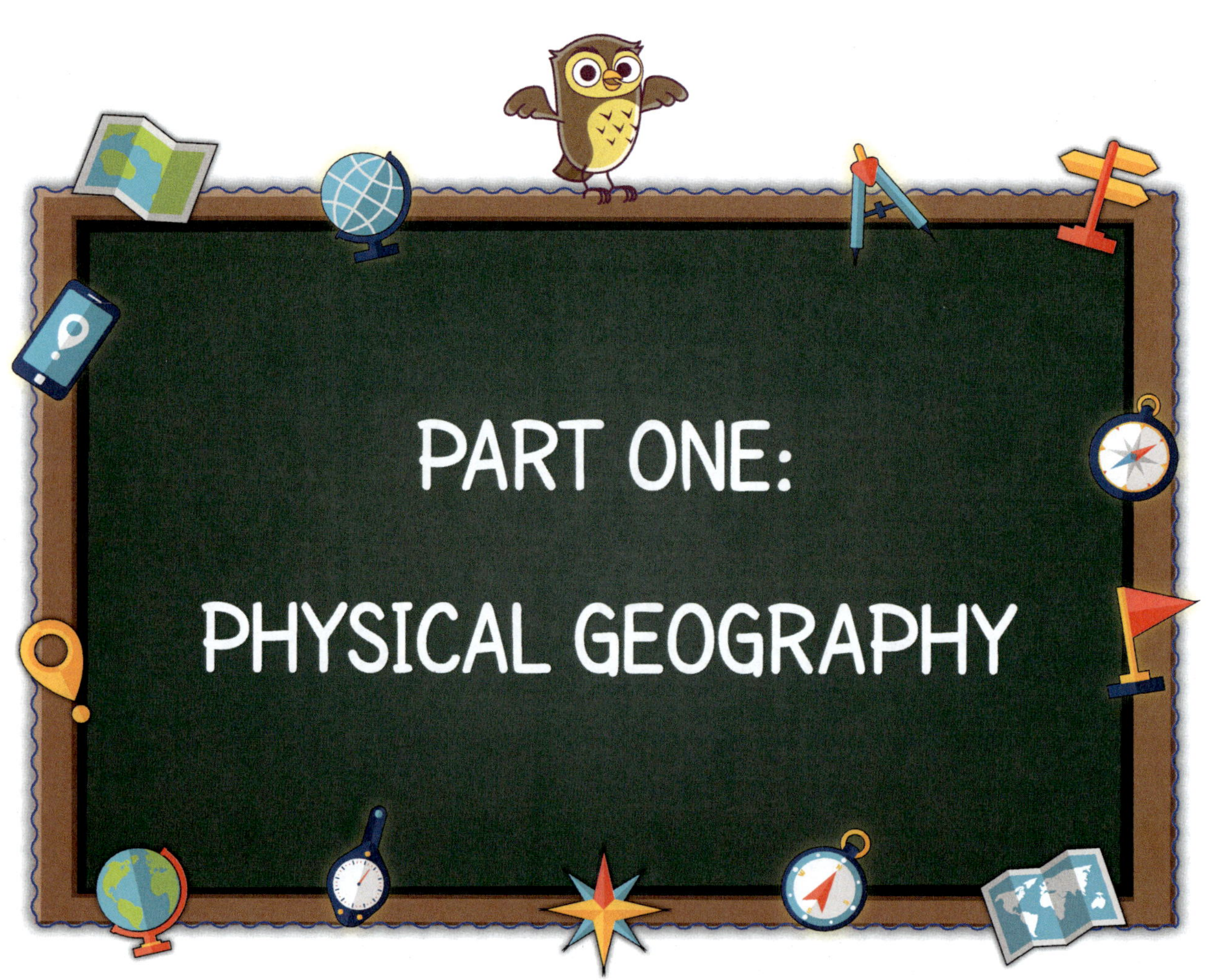

PART ONE:

PHYSICAL GEOGRAPHY

PANGÆA — ONE GIANT CONTINENT

Scientists estimate that the Earth is about 4.6 billion years old and was formed, along with the rest of the solar system, from a gas cloud that solidified.

About 300 million years ago, Earth didn't have seven continents. Instead, it had one massive supercontinent called Pangæa. Faults and rifts broke the land masses apart and pushed them away from each other. These land masses are part of huge tectonic plates that include both the continents and the seafloor. Tectonic plates cover the entire surface of the Earth like the plates on a turtle's shell. Those tectonic plates, with the continents, slowly moved across the Earth to their present positions. They continue to move today.

WHY IS THE EARTH ROUND?...OR IS IT?

When you see a picture of our Earth from space, it looks exactly like a round blue and white marble. But our Earth is not really 'round.' It is a shape called an 'ellipsoid,' which is kind of squatty and fat. The Earth is fatter in the middle than at both of the polar ends because Earth is constantly spinning and something called 'centrifugal force' pushes everything to the center of the planet's surface and outward. Isaac Newton first proposed that Earth was a sphere that is squashed at its poles and swollen at the equator. He was correct. Because of this bulge, the distance from Earth's center to sea level is roughly 13 miles greater at the equator than at the poles.

TECTONIC PLATES — THE SURFACE OF THE EARTH IS IN CONSTANT MOTION

The Earth is dynamic, which means it is constantly moving. The Earth's outer layer, or crust, is made up of about 20 massive, moving pieces called tectonic plates, which fit together like the pieces of a giant jigsaw puzzle. All of Earth's land and water sit on these plates. The plates are made of solid rock. Under the plates is a weaker layer of partially melted rock. The plates are constantly moving over this weaker layer, even though that movement is only a couple of centimeters per year. Although they move very slowly, they continually crash into, slide past, or sometimes slide under or over one another. In so doing, they form mountain ranges like the Himalayas and the Andes Mountains, and give rise to earthquakes. Forces deep within the Earth cause tectonic plates to constantly move slowly across the Earth's surface.

LATITUDE AND LONGITUDE — WHERE IN THE WORLD ARE YOU?

Lines of latitude and longitude are imaginary lines that circle our planet and give people a way of identifying and locating a specific point on the Earth.

LATITUDE — ARE YOU NORTH OR ARE YOU SOUTH?

Lines of **latitude** are *horizontal* lines that run east and west around the planet. They measure distances north and south of the **equator**. Since the equator is the starting point from which all other lines of latitude are measured, it is called 0^0 latitude. The latitude of all points north of the equator to the North Pole are called north latitude. Lines of latitude north of the equator are numbered from 1° to 90° N. The North Pole measures 90^0 N. The latitude of all points south of the equator to the South Pole are called south latitude. The South Pole measures 90^0 S. Lines of latitude south of the equator are numbered from 1° to 90° S.

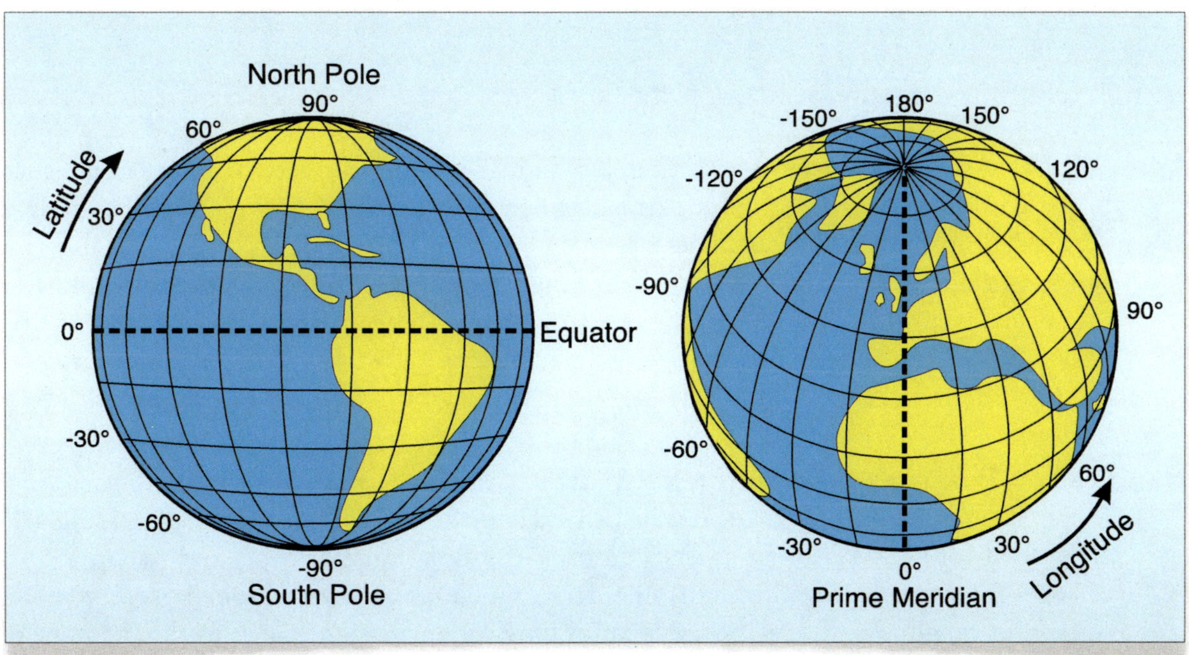

Because the lines of latitude are always the same distance apart, they are called **parallels**. The lines of latitude are not all equal in length, since they are each complete circles around the Earth that remain equidistant from each other. The lines of latitude vary in length from the longest at the equator to the shortest, which are just single points at the North and South Poles. Lines of latitude are measured in degrees (°). Degrees are further broken down into smaller units called minutes (') and seconds (").

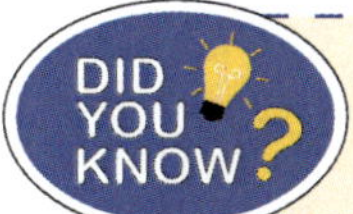

Deepest Underwater Trench: Mariana Trench, 200 miles southwest of Guam in the Pacific Ocean, 36,198 feet below the ocean surface.

There are other important lines of latitude besides the equator. For example, the Arctic Circle (66° 30' N) and the Antarctic Circle (66° 30' S) surround the cold regions around the North and South Poles. The area between the Tropic of Cancer (23° 27' N) and the Tropic of Capricorn (23° 27' S) is called the tropical zone or the tropics. It is known for its generally hot weather.

The **astrolabe**, a navigation device used for finding latitude of a point on the Earth, dates back as far as 120 B.C.E. and was the instrument of choice until about 1600 A.D. Sailors such as Columbus and Magellan relied on this tool during their journeys across the oceans. The mariner's astrolabe helped explorers and sailors figure out where they were north or south of the equator by measuring the angle and distance of the sun and stars above the horizon to determine local latitude.

LONGITUDE — ARE YOU EAST OR ARE YOU WEST?

While the astrolabe could measure latitude, there was no internationally recognized standard of measuring longitude, the distance east or west of a given point. As early as the 3rd Century B.C.E., Eratosthenes proposed a system of latitude and longitude for a map of the world. His prime meridian (line of longitude) passed through Alexandria and Rhodes. As time went on, a number of European maritime powers offered prizes for a method to determine longitude at sea. Spain was the first, offering a reward for a solution in 1567 and Holland offered 30,000 florins in the early 17th Century. However, neither of these prizes produced a solution.

The London observatory, at Greenwich, England, was set up in 1675 to address the longitude problem. In 1714, the British Parliament passed "An Act for Providing a Public Reward for such Person(s) as shall discover the Longitude at Sea," and set up a Board to administer the award. This led to the development of an internationally accepted series of lines of longitude. Today, the problem of longitude has been solved to the accuracy of one centimeter through satellite navigation.

Lines of **longitude** are vertical lines that run north and south and measure distances east and west of an imaginary line called the **prime meridian,** which runs through Greenwich, England. Since that is the point from which all other lines of longitude are measured, it is called 0^0 longitude. Since the Earth is a globe (360^0), the longitude of all points east of the prime meridian to a point halfway around the world (180^0) are called east longitude. All points west of the prime meridian to that same point halfway around the world (180^0) are called west longitude. The line that is exactly 180^0 in either direction from the prime meridian is called the **International Date Line**. Unlike lines of latitude, which are parallel to the equator, lines of longitude all meet at the north and south poles and are called **meridians**. All lines of longitude are of equal length and each equals one-half the circumference of the Earth because each extends from the North Pole to the South Pole.

FUN FACTS ABOUT THE INTERNATIONAL DATE LINE

- The date becomes one day later as you travel across the International Date Line in a western direction, and one day earlier as you travel across it in an eastern direction.
- The reason for this effect is that the International Date Line is, for the most part, about halfway around the world from Greenwich, England (the "prime meridian").
- Originally, the International Date Line ran along the 180° meridian. This was a relatively good choice, because most of the time, there is no land there. However, some problems arose when the 180° meridian crossed land areas.
- There are many groups of islands in the Pacific Ocean belonging to states that do not want some islands on one side of the date line and the rest on the other. Thus, they decided to move the date line, so that all islands are in the same time zone.
- The International Date Line is no longer a straight line. Some parts of it have been moved east or west to accommodate places such as the Aleutian Islands, Fiji, Tonga, Samoa, and New Zealand's Kermadec Islands to assure that they have the same date.

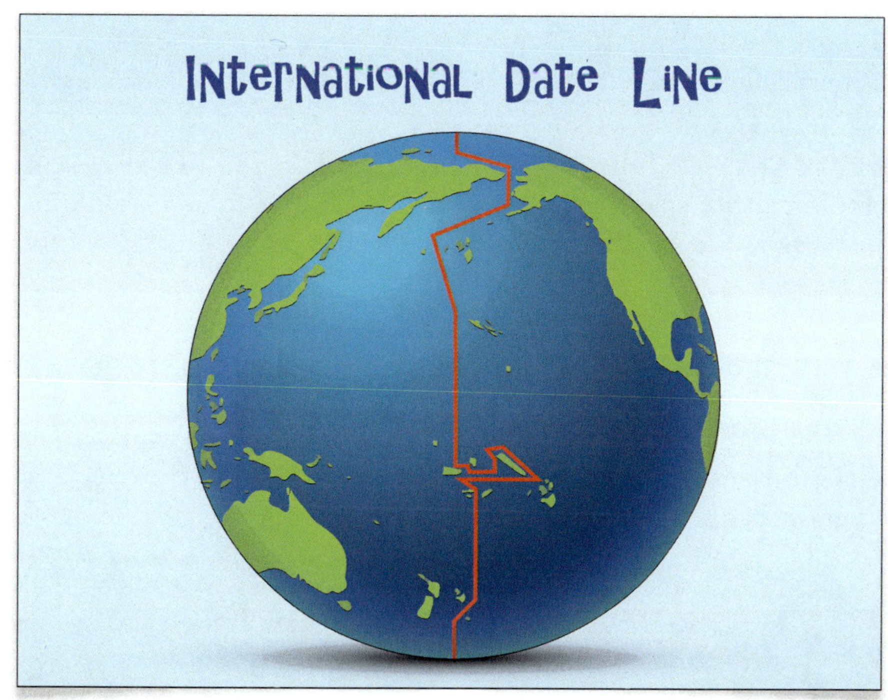

- Kiribati is a state consisting of many small islands spread over a huge portion of the Pacific. The 180⁰ meridian runs right through the state. Because Kiribati needed the same date all over its territory, the International Date Line swings far to the east, almost reaching the 150° meridian.

HOW LATITUDE AND LONGITUDE WORK TOGETHER

Latitude and longitude together can describe the exact location of any place on Earth. For example, Carmel, California, lies 36.5⁰ north of the equator and 121.9⁰ west of the prime meridian. These two numbers together are called **coordinates**.

THE POLES — THE ENDS OF THE EARTH

The Earth rotates or spins around an axis. If you were to draw an imaginary line at the axis through the center of the Earth, that line would exit the Earth in two places. At the top of the Earth, it would exit at the North Pole (90° north), and at the bottom it would exit at the South Pole (90° south).

The Earth's axis does not go straight up and down, but is tilted about 23½⁰. This tilting axis is what gives us seasons — and what causes it to be winter in the Southern Hemisphere when it is summer in the Northern Hemisphere and vice versa.

Imagine you are standing exactly on the North Pole. You pull out your compass. In what direction would the needle on the compass point? The answer may not be what you think. In order to answer this question, you will have to understand the difference between **True Geographic North** and **Magnetic North** because these two locations are completely different.

WHAT ARE THE GEOGRAPHIC (TRUE) NORTH AND SOUTH POLES?

The South and North Poles are directly opposite one another. The Geographic North and South Poles are where lines of longitude (meridians) converge at the north and south ends of the Earth.

Largest Sea: The Mediterranean Sea, 1,144,800 square miles.
The center of the Earth is hotter than the sun!

The North Pole is located in the middle of the Arctic Ocean. Scientists have tried marking the North Pole. Because the water here is permanently covered with moving sea ice, it is practically impossible to construct any type of permanent station at the true North Pole.

On the other side of the Earth, the South Pole lies on a **continental landmass** known as Antarctica. Because the ice on top of Antarctica moves only a few yards a year, the United States Antarctica program has installed a marker here to delineate the true South Pole.

THE GEOGRAPHIC NORTH POLE

The Geographic North Pole is located about 450 miles north of Greenland in the middle of the Arctic Ocean. This is called True North. The North Pole, at 90⁰ N, is the northernmost place on Earth. Most of the time, the North Pole is covered in sea ice.

In winter, temperatures average around minus 29⁰ F., but in the summer it is quite a bit warmer at plus 32⁰ F. These temperatures may sound pretty cold, but they are actually warmer than the average temperatures at the South Pole.

FUN FACTS ABOUT THE GEOGRAPHIC NORTH POLE

- The North Pole is not in any country. It is considered part of international waters.
- When you are standing on the North Pole, any direction you point to is South!
- During the summer, the sun is always above the horizon. The sun rises in March and sets in September, and then it is nighttime from September to March. That's a really long day and night!
- Peary and Henson are credited with being the first people to reach the North Pole. But were they really the first? Did indigenous people get there before them? And did they really get to the North Pole? The answer is still a mystery.

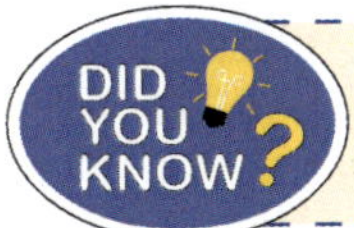

Istanbul is the only city in the world that is spread across two continents. 832 languages are currently spoken in Papua New Guinea.

THE GEOGRAPHIC SOUTH POLE

The Geographic South Pole is located at 90^0 south on the continent of Antarctica; it is at the southern end of the Earth's axis. Because the South Pole is on a glacier that shifts about 33 feet a year, the marker has to be relocated each year, using satellite positioning systems.

FUN FACTS ABOUT THE GEOGRAPHIC SOUTH POLE

- The first expedition of Europeans to the South Pole, led by Roald Amundsen, reached its goal on December 14, 1911. A second expedition, led by Robert Falcon Scott, reached the Pole just five weeks later, on January 18, 1912.
- Even though the North Pole and South Pole are "polar opposites," they both get the same amount of sunlight over the course of a year.
- Roald Amundsen, who flew over the North pole and the South Pole in an airship named the *Norge* in 1926, was the first person to see both Poles.

THE POLES ARE POLAR OPPOSITES IN OTHER WAYS TOO

- The Arctic is ocean surrounded by land. The Antarctic is land surrounded by ocean.
- The ocean under the Arctic ice is warmer than the ice itself, so the ocean warms the air a bit.
- The South Pole is about 50^0 F. colder than the North Pole.
- Antarctica is dry and has mountains. Its average elevation is about 7,500 feet and the higher you go, the colder it gets.
- Antarctica is actually a desert.

WHAT IS THE MAGNETIC NORTH POLE?

The Earth is one big magnet. The Magnetic North Pole is a point on Ellesmere Island in Northern Canada where the northern lines of attraction enter the Earth. When you pull out a compass, the movable needle aligns itself with the Earth's magnetic field. This means that a compass needle will point to the Magnetic North Pole which, as stated above, is different from the Geographic North Pole. The Magnetic North Pole is about 312 miles south of the Geographic North Pole.

The Magnetic North Pole is actually moving. This phenomenon is known as the **Polar Shift Theory**. The planet we live on is dynamic. Earth is changing every day. Plate tectonics push continents apart, sea levels fluctuate up and down, and volcanoes erupt, discharging ash and smoke. Over the last 150 years, the North Magnetic Pole has crept north over 625 miles. Scientists suggest it migrates about 6 miles per year and can even flip from pole-to-pole.

WHY DOES THE EARTH HAVE A MAGNETIC FIELD?

Imagine the Earth has a big magnetic bar running through it, and the magnetic poles are located at the north and south ends of the big bar. While there is no actual magnetic bar inside the Earth, there are massive currents of molten iron minerals deep below the Earth's surface that act like a magnet to create the Earth's magnetic field and determine where the Magnetic North Pole and Magnetic South Pole are located. This magnetic field allows us to use the magnets in a compass to find our way and make sure we are heading in the right direction.

The **Magnetic South Pole** is in the Antarctic Ocean and not even located on Antarctica! It is the southern pole of the Earth's magnetic field and is at the point on the Earth where a compass needle, which is able to move vertically as well as horizontally, points straight up and away from the Earth's surface.

THE COMPASS — HOW WE GET FROM HERE TO THERE

A **compass** is an extremely important instrument used for navigation and orientation. It shows direction relative to the geographic cardinal directions of north, south, east, and west on the compass face. In their earliest navigational use, compasses served as backups for when the Sun, stars, or other landmarks could not be seen. Eventually, as compasses became more reliable and explorers understood how to read them, they became a critical navigational tool.

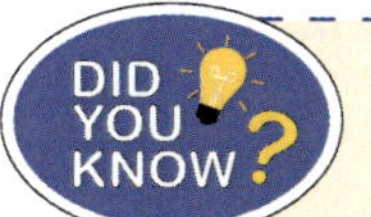

Highest Lake: The highest navigable lake is Lake Titicaca in Peru, 12,500 feet above sea level.

FUN FACTS ABOUT COMPASSES

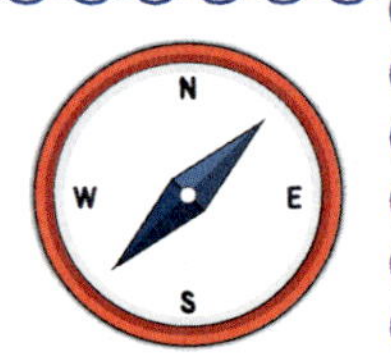

- The Chinese first used compasses not for navigation, but to orient and organize buildings and other structures according to *feng shui*, the ancient practice of harmonizing an environment according to the "laws of Heaven."
- The compass is one of the Four Great Inventions from ancient China, and was first used during the Han Dynasty between 20 B.C.E. and 20 A.D.

THE EARTH'S HEMISPHERES — IF A HEMISPHERE IS HALF THE EARTH, HOW COME THERE ARE FOUR HEMISPHERES?

A hemisphere is half of the Earth (*hemi* = half; *sphere* = sphere). The Earth can actually be divided into hemispheres in two ways. First, by the equator, that imaginary line around the center of the Earth. This line divides the Earth into the Northern and Southern Hemispheres. Second, by the prime meridian, which is 0^{0} longitude, and another meridian at 180^{0}. These lines of longitude divide the Earth into the Eastern and Western Hemispheres.

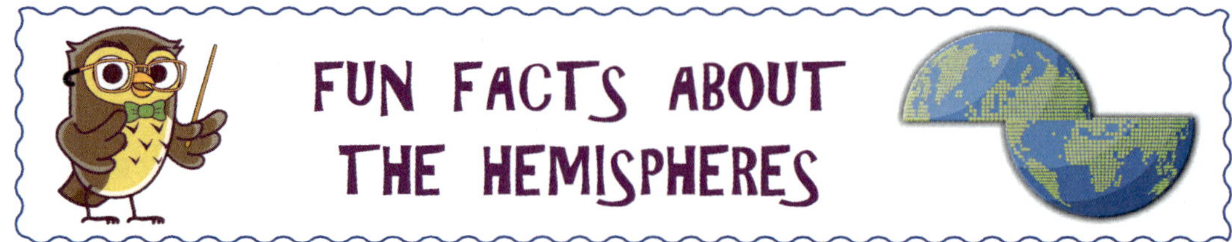

- The Northern Hemisphere contains almost 90% of the Earth's land and the Southern Hemisphere contains 90% of its water. Most of the world's population lives in the Northern Hemisphere.
- When it is summer in the Northern Hemisphere, it is winter in the Southern Hemisphere.

- The hemispheres have something in common: the Sun rises in the East and sets in the West in both hemispheres, since the Earth rotates counterclockwise on its axis, or from West to East.

WHAT CAUSES THE SEASONS?

We divide the year into four seasons: spring, summer, autumn or fall, and winter. Each season lasts 3 months with summer being the warmest season, winter being the coldest, and spring and autumn lying in between. Seasons are caused because the Earth travels (orbits) around the Sun, once a year (every 365¼ days). As the Earth orbits the Sun, the amount of sunlight each location on the planet gets every day changes slightly. This change causes the seasons.

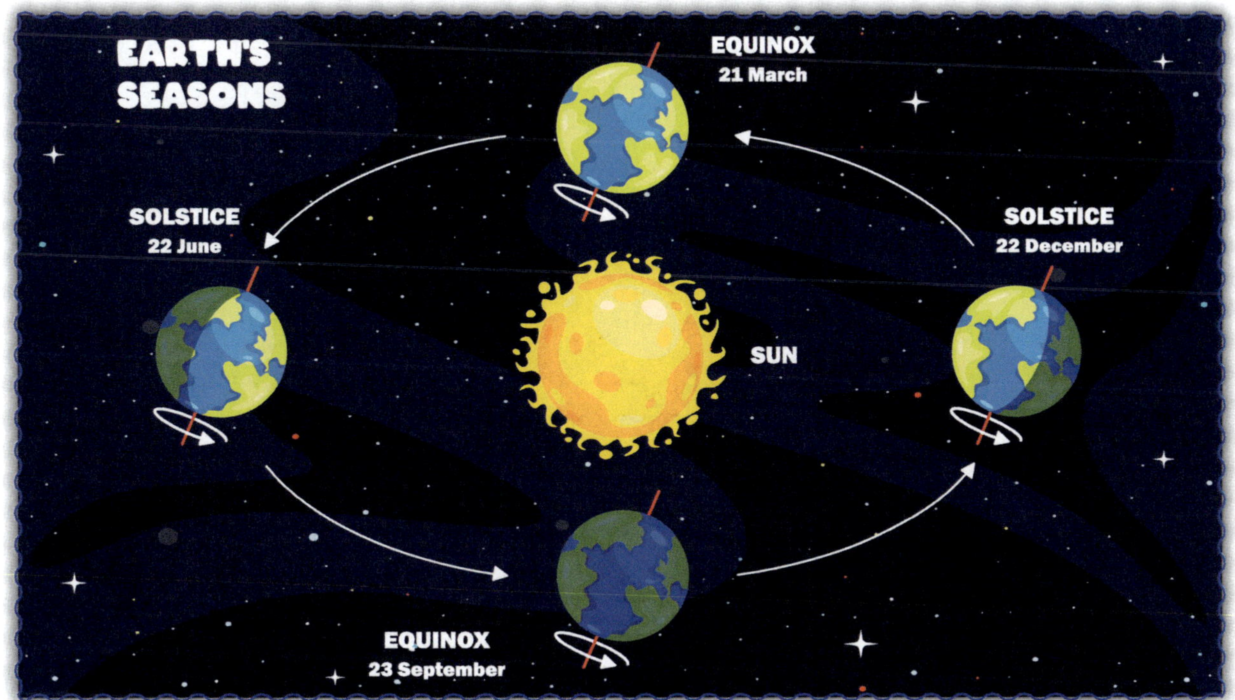

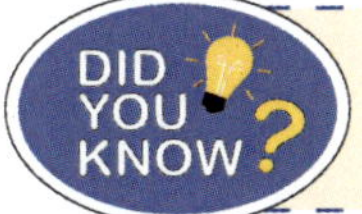

Russia spans 11 time zones. At one end of Russia it could be 7 in the morning and at the other it's 6 in the evening.

The Earth moves in two ways: not only does it revolve (orbit) around the Sun every year but it also rotates on its own axis, making one complete turn each 24 hours. This Earth's rotation is why we have day and night. However, the Earth doesn't rotate in a straight up and down manner relative to the Sun. It is slightly tilted. In scientific terms, the Earth is tilted $23\frac{1}{2}^0$ from its path, or orbital plane, around the Sun.

The Earth is like a spinning top moving in an orbit around the Sun. The spinning Earth leans over in its orbit, always tilting the same way. When the Earth is on one side of the Sun, the tilt leans the Northern Hemisphere toward the Sun. Half a year later, when the Earth is on the other side of the Sun, the Southern Hemisphere leans toward the Sun. In the hemisphere leaning toward the Sun, the Sun rises high in the sky and the days are long and hot; it is summer. In the hemisphere leaning away from the Sun, the Sun rises lower in the sky and the days are short; it is winter. For this reason, seasons north of the equator are the opposite of seasons south of the equator. When it's winter in Europe and the United States, it is summer in Australia and South Africa.

LONGEST AND SHORTEST DAYS

In the Northern Hemisphere, the longest day (or **summer solstice**) occurs around June 21st while the longest night (or **winter solstice**) is around December 21st. It is just the opposite in the Southern Hemisphere, where the longest day takes place around December 21st and the longest night is around June 21st. The word **solstice** derives from the Latin *sōlstitium*, which comes from the parts *sōl*, "sun," and *sistere*, "to stand still." Solstitium translates to "the standing still of the Sun."

An **equinox** occurs when the position of the sun is exactly over the equator. When this happens, the hours of daylight and the hours of darkness are about equal almost everywhere on Earth. Equinoxes take place twice a year. **Equinox** comes from the Latin words *aequi*, which means "equal," and *nox*, which means "night." — the day and night are of equal length.

The **autumnal (or fall) equinox** occurs around September 23rd in the Northern Hemisphere and around March 21st in the Southern Hemisphere. Autumn, or Fall, begins with the autumnal equinox. After the autumnal equinox, the days become shorter and the nights become longer.

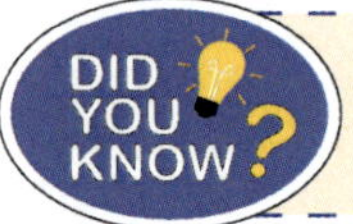

Deepest Ocean: Pacific Ocean, average depth 13,215 feet.
Smallest Ocean: Arctic Ocean, 5,427,000 square miles.

The **vernal (or spring) equinox** marks the beginning of Spring. After the vernal equinox, the days become longer and the nights become shorter. The vernal equinox occurs around March 21st in the Northern Hemisphere and around September 23rd in the Southern Hemisphere.

MAPS AND CHARTS — PUTTING PEN TO PAPER AND MAKING SENSE OF IT ALL

Cartography is the study of maps and charts. **Maps** apply to land and **charts** are for marine areas. People have been making maps since prehistoric times. The oldest known map is not of the Earth but of the stars. In 2000, a map of the night sky was discovered in one of the caves at Lascaux, France. That map is believed to be more than 16,500 years old!

A **map** is a drawing of all or part of the Earth's surface. Its basic purpose is to show where things are located. Maps may show visible features, such as rivers and lakes, forests, buildings, and roads, as well as things that cannot be seen, such as boundaries, elevations, populations, and temperatures.

The first maps were made by hand with brushes and parchment and used simple instruments and mathematical equations. As time passed, the magnetic compass, and much later, magnetic storage devices, allowed maps to be far more accurate and gave us the ability to store and manipulate them digitally. Today's mapmaking is very precise, thanks to satellite images and the Global Positioning System known as GPS.

THE DIFFERENCE BETWEEN A MAP AND A GLOBE

Maps are drawn on a flat, one-dimensional surface. A map displayed on a three-dimensional spherical surface is called a **globe**.

No map is perfect because it is impossible to accurately represent the curved surface of the Earth on a flat piece of paper. This inaccuracy is because any rounded surface must be distorted when shown on a flat surface. But while a globe is more accurate, it is more difficult to carry around. Because of this, flat maps are much more useful and practical when you study the Earth.

The most familiar kinds of maps are physical and political maps.

Physical maps, also known as **topographic maps**, show the location and shape of features on the Earth's surface. These often include natural features, such as mountains and lakes. They may also include things that humans have built, such as roads and railroads.

Political maps show the boundaries of countries, states, provinces, counties, and cities. Most maps combine features of both topographic and political maps. A book of maps is known as an **atlas**.

FIVE ELEMENTS OF ANY MAP

Maps contain lots of information. Most maps will have the five following things: a Title, a Legend, a Grid, a Compass Rose to indicate direction, and a Scale.

- **Title** tells you what is being represented on the map (e.g., Carmel, California).
- **Legend** (also known as **the key**) explains the symbols used on the map for various features like mountains or rivers and other major landmarks.
- **Grid** is made up of longitude and latitude lines to precisely indicate specific locations.
- **Compass Rose** shows the cardinal directions of North, South, East, and West as it relates to the map.
- **Scale** provides a ratio of the distance on a map to actual distance on land: (e.g., 1 inch = 10 miles).

Knowing about these five elements on a map will help you better understand the information you're looking at when using maps.

THE WATER CYCLE — WATER, WATER EVERYWHERE

About 71% of the Earth's surface is covered in water. The oceans hold about 97% of all Earth's water. Water also exists in the air as water vapor, in clouds, in rivers and lakes, in icecaps and glaciers, in the ground as soil moisture in aquifers, and in every living organism.

The Earth has been recycling water for over 4 billion years! *There is not one drop more or one drop less of water on Earth now than when the Earth was first formed.* The water you drink today could be the same water the dinosaurs splashed in 63 million years ago.

The world's water moves between lakes, rivers, oceans, the atmosphere, and the land in an ongoing cycle called the **water cycle**. As it goes through this continuous system, it can be a liquid (water), a gas (vapor) or a solid (ice). Here are the main stages in the water cycle:

EVAPORATION

Energy from the sun heats up the surface of the Earth, causing the temperature of the water in our rivers, lakes, and oceans to rise. When this happens, some of the water **evaporates** into the air, turning into a gaseous state known as vapor. Plants and trees also lose water to the atmosphere through their leaves. This process is known as **transpiration**.

CONDENSATION

As water vapor rises up high into the sky, it cools and turns back into a liquid, forming clouds. This process is called **condensation**. Currents high up in the air move these clouds around the globe.

PRECIPITATION

When too much water has condensed, the water droplets in the clouds become too big and heavy for the air to hold them. And so they fall back down to Earth as rain, snow, hail, or sleet. This is a process known as **precipitation**.

Largest Island: Greenland, 839,999 square miles.
Largest Peninsula: Arabia, 1,250,000 square miles..

COLLECTION

- The fallen precipitation is then **collected** in bodies of water, such as rivers, lakes, oceans, and aquifers from where it will eventually evaporate back into the air, beginning the cycle all over again. *How* it is collected depends on where it lands.Some water will fall directly into lakes, rivers, or the sea.
- If the water falls on vegetation, it may evaporate from leaves back into the air, or it may trickle down into the ground. Some of this water may then be taken up by the plant roots in the Earth.
- In cold climates, the precipitation may build up on land as snow, ice, or glaciers. If temperatures rise, the ice will melt to liquid water and then soak into the ground, or flow into rivers or the ocean.
- Some of this precipitation is consumed by animals, including people.

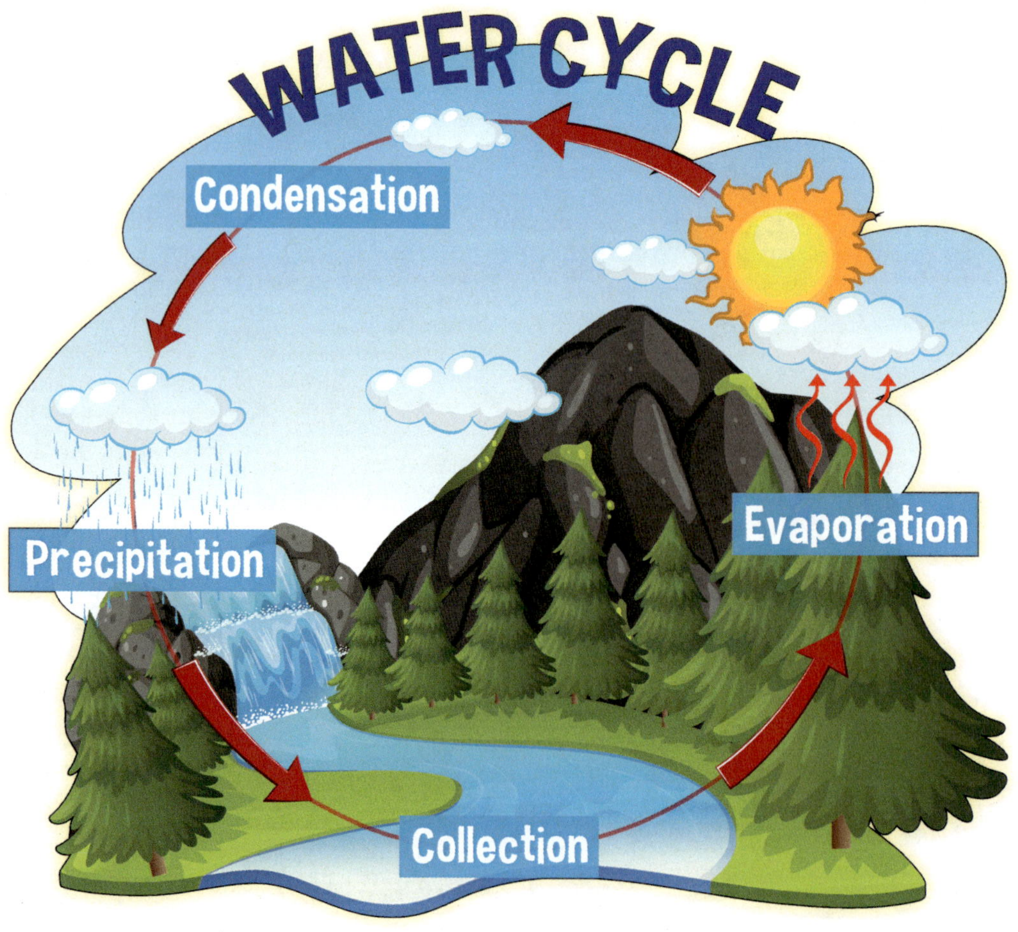

Water that reaches land directly may flow across the ground and collect in the oceans, rivers, or lakes. This water is called **surface run-off.** Some precipitation will instead soak or **infiltrate** into the soil and collect in an **aquifer**, an underground saturated soil or rock layer below the land surface, from where it will slowly move through the ground until eventually reaching a river or the ocean. And then the whole process begins again because it is a never-ending cycle!

The human body contains a lot of water. In fact, humans are almost 60% water. Remember that every drop of water on Earth has been here since the Earth formed. That means that 60% of you is made up of water drops that were once in a cloud, or the ocean, or an underground aquifer, or maybe even inside a dinosaur! We are all a part of the ongoing water cycle!

EROSION — THE EARTH'S SANDPAPER

Erosion is the wearing away of the land by forces such as water, wind, and ice. Erosion has formed virtually all of the Earth's surface features, including mountain peaks, valleys, and coastlines. Many different forces in nature cause erosion. Depending on the type of force, erosion can happen quickly or take thousands of years. Wind, the force of gravity, and floodwaters move soil far from its original location. Rivers and streams create a significant amount of erosion over time by breaking up particles along river bottoms and carrying them downstream. The most visibly spectacular illustration of river erosion, and certainly the most famous natural phenomenon in the United States, is the Grand Canyon of the Colorado River in Arizona.

Human activity can accelerate the pace of erosion by causing excessive losses of topsoil. The damming of rivers, the plowing of fields, and the cutting down of forests are all examples of human activity that result in erosion. Planting hedges, trees, and buffer vegetation around farmland to protect it from the wind, moving herds around so that grasslands will grow back, and planting new trees to replace the ones cut down are examples of productive efforts to limit the amount of erosion caused by human activity.

DID YOU KNOW?

Largest Archipelago: Indonesia, 3,500-mile stretch of 17,000 islands.
More than 20 % of Earth's oxygen supply is produced by the Amazon Rainforest.

FUN FACTS ABOUT EROSION

- The word erosion comes from the Latin word *erosionem* which means "a gnawing away."
- The Colorado River has been eroding the Grand Canyon for millions of years.
- Erosion by wind can cause huge dust storms.
- Fossils in sedimentary rock are often uncovered by erosion.

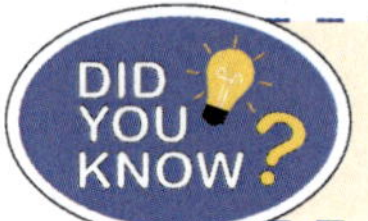

Largest Gorge: Grand Canyon, Colorado River, Arizona, U.S., 217 miles long, 4-18 miles wide, 1 mile deep.

GLACIERS — THE EARTH'S ICY BULLDOZERS

Approximately two-thirds of the world's fresh water, as opposed to saltwater, occurs in the form of ice. Most of that frozen water is found on the continent of Antarctica in the form of glaciers.

A **glacier** is a mass of ice and snow that stays frozen throughout the year. When enough snow builds up, the weight of the snow compresses and turns into solid ice. It can take hundreds of years for a large glacier to form.

A glacier moves about 150 feet per year, which can vary greatly with climate change. This is one of the reasons why global climate change is such a critical issue today. When a glacier moves across the land, it acts like a giant bulldozer, pushing and collecting rock, dirt, and debris. When glaciers reach the sea, chunks break off into the water and remain afloat as icebergs.

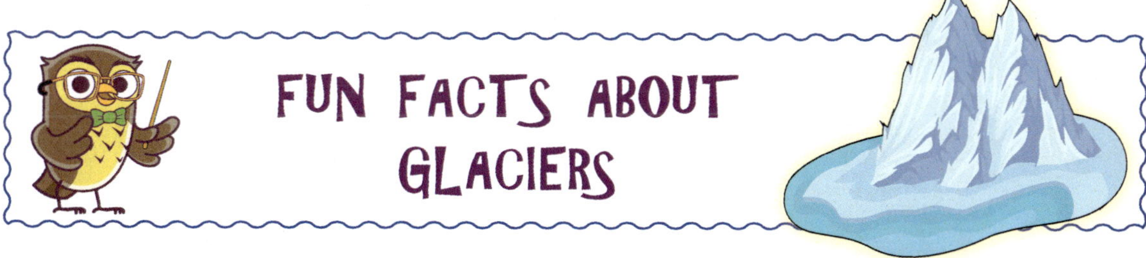

- Most glaciers are located near the North or South Poles, but glaciers also exist high in mountain ranges, such as the Himalayas and the Andes.
- When icebergs fall off glaciers into the water, we say the glaciers are **calving.**
- **The glacier head** is where the glacier starts. The **terminus**, at the end of the glacier, is also called **the glacier foot**.
- A **moraine** is a deposit of rock and dirt carried by a glacier and left behind once the glacier melts and recedes.
- Most of Greenland is covered with a giant icecap, a glacier nearly two miles thick in some areas.
- Sometimes glaciers move much faster than normal. This is called **glacial surge.**
- The fastest known glacier moved over seven miles in just three months.
- Glaciers are capable of carving and eroding rock with their weight and slow, steady movement. Glaciers that existed a long time ago are responsible for stunning landscapes, like Yosemite National Park in California.
- At over 125 miles long, the Bering Glacier in Alaska is the longest glacier in the United States.

CLIMATE AND WEATHER — CLIMATE IS WHAT WE EXPECT, WEATHER IS WHAT WE GET!

Every day, most of us watch the weather forecast on television, turn on our computer, or flip to an app on our cell phone to find out whether it will be raining in Seattle, snowing in Colorado ski country, or a day filled with warm sunshine in Athens, Greece.

Weather describes the conditions outside right now in a specific place. For example, if you see that it's raining outside, that's a way to describe today's weather. Rain, snow, wind, hurricanes, and tornadoes are all weather events.

Climate, on the other hand, is more than just one or two rainy days. Climate describes the weather conditions that are expected in a region at a particular time of year. Is it usually rainy or usually dry? Is it typically hot or typically cold? A region's climate is determined by observing its weather over a period of many years — generally 30 years or more. So, for example, one or two weeks of rainy **weather** wouldn't change the fact that Phoenix, Arizona, typically has a dry, desert **climate**.

WHAT IS CLIMATE CHANGE?

Our Earth is surrounded by an atmosphere made up of gases. When sunlight enters our atmosphere, some of the sun's heat is trapped by the gas, and some bounces back out into space. By trapping that heat, our atmosphere keeps Earth warm enough to live on. Without it, our planet would be very cold, like Mars, and it would be impossible for human beings to live on Earth.

Climate change describes a change in the average conditions — such as temperature and rainfall — in a region over a long period of time. For example, 20,000 years ago, much of the United States was covered in glaciers. In the United States today, we have a warmer climate and fewer glaciers. Global climate change refers to the average long-term changes over the entire Earth. These include warming (or cooling) temperatures and changes in precipitation.

Earth's climate has always naturally cycled through change, caused by how much of the sun's energy was absorbed by the atmosphere. Over the past 650,000 years, Earth has gone through seven ice ages, when the temperature dropped significantly and a lot of the world was covered in ice glaciers. Each time, the planet eventually warmed up and melted the ice.

Most of these changes are a natural part of Earth's 4.5 billion-year history. They are due to tiny variations in the Earth's orbit, which alters the amount of solar energy reaching the planet.

GLOBAL WARMING — WHEN EVEN THE SHADOWS NEED SHADOWS TO COOL OFF

Today, most scientists are very concerned by a phenomenon called **global warming**. Global warming is the term used to describe the rising of the average temperature on Earth.

Even small variations of the planet's average temperature can have a large impact on the environment. For example, the ice ages that occurred in the past generally involved a reduction in the global temperature of around 41° F. In recent times, the Earth's average temperature has increased about 1.5° F. in the past 100 years. That doesn't sound like much, but scientists expect the climate will warm another 0.5° F. to 8.5 ° F. by the year 2100.

Here are a few things that scientists think may happen as the Earth's temperature rises. Some of these are already happening.

- Glaciers are melting: Melting polar ice caps and glaciers are causing huge chunks of ice to fall into the oceans. The melting ice is causing sea levels to rise about 1/8 of an inch per year. Some scientists predict that if sea levels continue to rise at current rates, this could cause flooding in cities located near the coast and entire cities may be submerged in the next 100 years.
- In warm, dry regions, increased temperatures are causing severe drought. Global warming has also led to coral bleaching of nearly two-thirds of Australia's Great Barrier Reef. The corals provide a habitat for nearly 1,500 different species of fish. This loss of sea life also affects hundreds of millions of humans who rely on marine creatures for food.
- Migration of animals: Animals will migrate to cooler spots as their old habitats get too warm. This could upset the food chain and put some species in danger of extinction.
- Extreme weather: Some scientists think that warming will fuel more powerful hurricanes as well as more droughts, wildfires, and flooding in different areas of the world.
- Change in ecosystems: Cold weather biomes, such as the tundra, will shrink, while deserts will continue to expand.

WHAT'S DIFFERENT ABOUT THE CURRENT GLOBAL WARMING?

Ninety-seven percent of climate scientists say that recent changes in Earth's climate are not due to natural causes and that there is a direct connection between human activity and the changes occurring on our planet. Over the past 150 years, humans have used more and more engines, vehicles, and other machines. These devices burn fossil fuels like coal and oil, which emit carbon dioxide (CO2), methane (CH4), ozone (O3), chlorofluorocarbons (CFCs), sulfur dioxide (SO2), and other gases. These gases in the atmosphere end up trapping that heat. We call them "**greenhouse gases**" because they turn the planet into a giant, warm greenhouse. It is these greenhouse gases created by human activities that are causing our planet to warm at a faster rate than ever recorded before.

Normally, plants, trees, and the oceans absorb carbon dioxide and release it back into the atmosphere as oxygen. But an increase in fossil fuels has created more carbon dioxide than nature can take in. Deforestation and the destruction of habitats also reduce the number of trees and plants. That makes it even harder to absorb all that carbon dioxide.

When too much carbon dioxide remains in the atmosphere, it causes problems for Earth's climate. Sunlight can pass through those gases, but the heat the Sun generates cannot escape back into space. So the gases end up trapping that heat. This then turns the planet into a giant greenhouse. This **greenhouse effect** leads to changes in the climate, like increased temperatures.

WHAT CAN WE DO ABOUT IT?

You can do a lot! It's simple to make a difference to keep the Earth healthy. Try some of these tips to reduce the amount of carbon dioxide you add to the atmosphere.

- Instead of traveling in a car, use public transportation, walk, or ride your bike when you can. Biking or walking 10 miles each day instead of riding in a car can save up to 1.9 tons of carbon dioxide from entering the atmosphere every year.
- Reduce and reuse things as much as possible. Factories emit lots of carbon dioxide when making new products. Fix your appliances and clothes instead of buying new products.
- Wash your clothes in cold water, and hang them outside to dry.
- Electronics use energy even when they're turned off, so unplug them when you're not using them. It could save your family about $200 a year on its energy bill.
- Eat less meat and dairy. Farm animals emit methane, a heat-trapping gas. Livestock account for almost half of the world's heat-trapping gas emissions.
- Buy locally grown and in-season foods and products to reduce emissions from transporting products.
- Wear a warm sweater at home in the winter instead of turning up the heat, and open your windows instead of blasting the air conditioning in the summer.

NATURAL WEATHER PHENOMENA

HURRICANES — A LOT OF WIND

Hurricanes are giant tropical storms that produce heavy rainfall and *super*-strong winds. They form over warm ocean waters near the equator, using these warm waters as an energy source. Hurricanes rotate around a circular center called the **eye,** where it is generally calm with no clouds. Surrounding the eye is the eye wall — the most dangerous part of the hurricane with the strongest winds, thickest clouds and heaviest rain. Most hurricanes occur harmlessly out at sea. However, when they move toward land, they can be incredibly dangerous and cause serious damage. The strong spiraling winds of a hurricane can reach speeds of up to 190 mph, strong enough to rip up entire trees and destroy buildings.

Hurricanes are also called **cyclones** and **typhoons**, depending on where they occur. In the Atlantic Ocean and Northeast Pacific, they are called hurricanes; in the Northwest Pacific, they are called typhoons and, in the South Pacific and Indian Ocean, they are called cyclones. In the Southern Hemisphere, hurricanes rotate in a clockwise direction, and in the northern hemisphere, they rotate in a counterclockwise direction. This is due to what's called the **coriolis effect**, which is produced by the Earth's rotation.

FUN FACTS ABOUT HURRICANES

- The word hurricane comes from "Huracan," the name of a Mayan god. The Mayans believed this was the god of big winds and evil spirits.
- When a hurricane reaches land, it often produces a **storm surge.** This takes place when high winds drive the sea toward the shore, causing water levels to rise and creating large, crashing waves. Storm surges can reach up to 20 feet and extend inland to over 90 miles.
- The largest hurricane/typhoon on record is Typhoon Tip, which occurred in 1979 in the Northwest Pacific. With a diameter of around 1,400 miles, it was nearly half the size of the United States!
- In 1970, the world's deadliest hurricane/cyclone, the Bhola Cyclone, which struck Bangladesh, killed over 300,000 people.
- In 2005, Hurricane Katrina killed over 1,800 people in the United States and caused $80 billion worth of property damage. Eighty percent of the city of New Orleans was flooded.

- Hurricanes are given names by the **World Meteorological Organization** (WMO) so that they can be distinguished. Each year, tropical storms are named in alphabetical order according to a list produced by the WMO. That name stays with the storm if it develops into a hurricane. The names can only be repeated after six years.

TORNADOES — C'MON, BABY, LET'S DO THE TWIST!

A **tornado** is a rapidly spinning tube of air that touches both the ground and a cloud above. It is only a tornado if it touches the ground. If it does not touch the ground, the storm is known as a **funnel**. Tornadoes occur on every continent of the world. In the Southern Hemisphere, tornadoes usually rotate in a clockwise direction. In the Northern Hemisphere, they usually rotate in a counterclockwise direction. Most tornadoes have wind speeds of less than 100 miles per hour. Extreme tornadoes can reach wind speeds of over 300 miles per hour. Most tornadoes travel a few miles before exhausting themselves.

- A tornado that occurs over water is often called a **waterspout**.
- Tornadoes are sometimes called **twisters**.

- The **Fujita Scale** is a common way of measuring the strength of tornadoes. The scale ranges from F0 tornadoes that cause minimal damage to F5 tornadoes that cause massive damage.
- The fastest winds on Earth occur inside tornadoes.
- The USA averages around 1,200 tornadoes every year, more than any other country. The majority of these tornadoes occur in a geographically unique area in the center of the United States nicknamed "Tornado Alley."
- In 1989, the deadliest tornado ever recorded in the world killed around 1,300 people in Bangladesh.

WHAT IS THE DIFFERENCE BETWEEN A TORNADO AND A HURRICANE?

- A hurricane can be as wide as 400 miles from side to side.
- A tornado is much smaller, with a diameter of no more than 50 yards.
- A hurricane has a small area in the center, known as "the eye of the storm," which is calm. If you are in the center, or eye, of a hurricane, there is dead calm and a blue sky above you.
- A tornado has a center core of violent ascending currents of air. The center of the tornado is the most dangerous part.
- A hurricane forms first at sea and can move toward the land.
- Tornadoes are formed on land.

MONSOONS

A **monsoon**, which is a large sea breeze, occurs when the wind blows from the cooler ocean to the much warmer land mass. Contrary to popular belief, monsoon does not necessarily mean rain. Monsoons can also include dry phases. Monsoons are typically associated with rainy seasons in the tropics. In several parts of the world, life depends on the monsoon rains. When the monsoon doesn't occur in these places, it can result in extensive famine and death of both humans and animals.

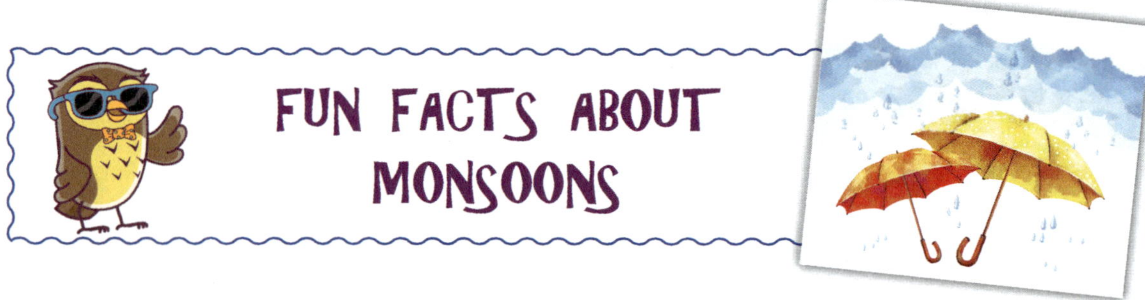

- The name "monsoon" is believed to be derived from the Arabic word *mausim*, which means "a shift in season or wind."
- Arizona receives 31.5% of its total annual rainfall during a monsoon. In Arizona, during the monsoon season, it is common to see a wall of dust that reaches hundreds of feet in the air.
- There are nearly 500,000 lightning strikes during a monsoon.
- India experiences the most dramatic monsoons in the world.

TSUNAMIS — MORE THAN BIG WAVES

Tsunamis are huge waves of water that are usually caused by earthquakes, underwater landslides, or volcanic eruptions. Although they are sometimes referred to as tidal waves, this term has fallen out of favor because tsunamis are not related to tides. As a tsunami approaches the shore, water may recede from the coast. If it is shallow enough, the water

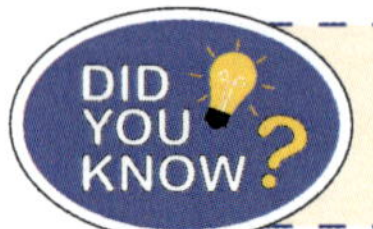

The Appalachian mountains are shrinking, due to erosion.
The Himalayas are still growing today, by about 0.78 inches a year.

may be pulled back hundreds of yards. Out in the open ocean, tsunami waves are only about three feet high because the water is deep. However, as the water becomes shallow, the waves slow down and begin to grow. Now they can rise as high as 115 feet. The scariest thing about a tsunami is its **wavelength**, as this determines how far inland it can travel. Whereas a large wave caused by a storm might have a wavelength of up to 500 feet, a tsunami could reach up to a fearsome 3,000 feet! Tsunamis can travel at speeds of 500 miles an hour, almost as fast as a jet plane.

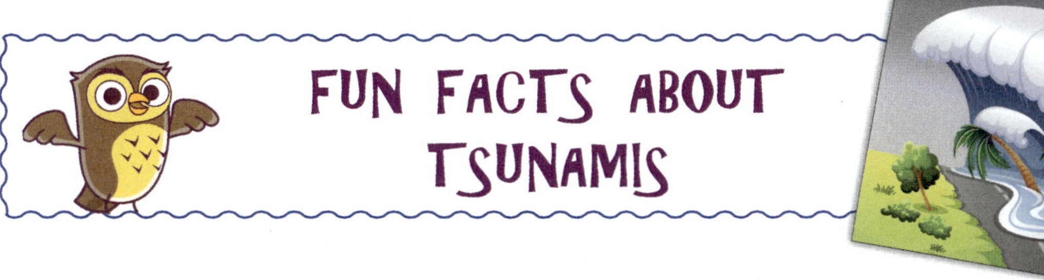

- The Japanese word *tsunami* literally means "harbor wave."
- About four out of five tsunamis happen within the **Ring of Fire**, a zone in the Pacific Ocean where earthquakes and volcanic eruptions frequently take place.
- The Hawaiian Islands are always at great risk for a tsunami — they get about one per year and a severe one every seven years. The biggest tsunami that occurred in Hawaii happened in 1946. The coast of Hilo Island was hit with 30-ft. waves at 500 mph.
- When tsunamis hit shallow water (often near the coast), they slow down but increase in height.
- An earthquake in the Indian Ocean off Indonesia in December 2004 caused a tsunami that killed over 200,000 people in 14 countries.
- To save lives, scientists established the **Pacific Tsunami Warning System**, based in Hawaii. Its network of detectors can track quakes that may cause a tsunami. These waves can race from one side of the Pacific Ocean to the other in less than a day, so people need to be warned in time to head for higher ground!

EARTHQUAKES — WHOLE LOTTA SHAKIN' GOING ON

Earthquakes usually occur on the edges of large sections of the Earth's crust called **tectonic plates**. These plates are slowly and continuously moving over earth's surface. The edges, or boundaries, of these tectonic plates interact where they collide, pull apart, or slide past each other. The plate boundaries can get stuck, but the plates keep moving. Pressure slowly starts to build up where the edges are stuck and, once the pressure gets strong enough, the plates will suddenly, move causing an earthquake.

About a half-million quakes rock the Earth every day. People don't feel most of them because the quakes are too small, too far below the surface, or deep on the seafloor. Some, however, are so powerful they can be felt thousands of miles away.

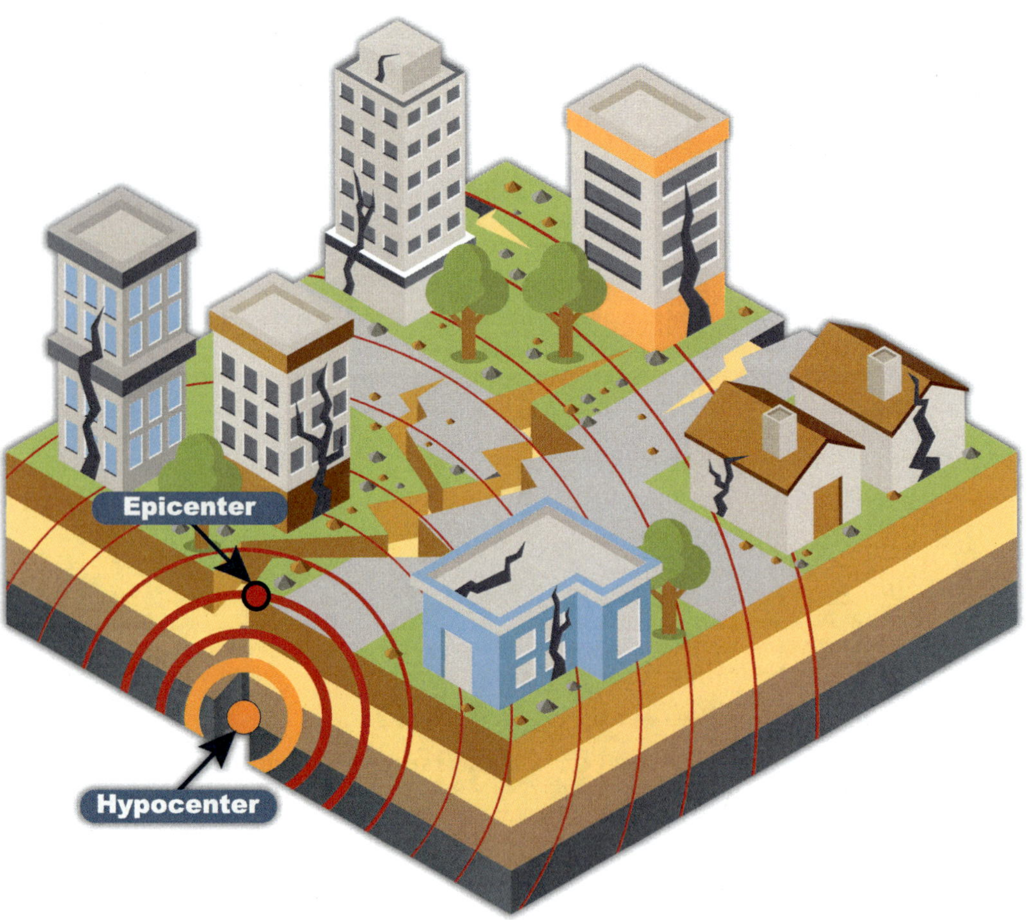

A powerful earthquake can cause landslides, tsunamis, flooding, and other catastrophic events. Most damage and deaths from earthquakes happen in populated areas. That's because the shaking can cause windows to break, structures to collapse, fire, and other dangers. **Geologists**, scientists who study the Earth, cannot predict earthquakes yet, but they continue to study earthquakes to better understand them and hopefully, to be able to someday predict when they will occur.

FUN FACTS ABOUT EARTHQUAKES

- The Richter scale, invented by Charles Richter in 1935, rates the amount of energy released from a single earthquake, letting us know the strength of the earthquake.
- A **seismograph** is what scientists use to measure the earthquake on the Richter scale.
- The place where the earthquake starts, below the surface of the Earth, is called the **hypocenter** or focus. The place directly above the hypocenter on the surface of the Earth is called the **epicenter.** The earthquake will be strongest at this point on the surface.
- The shaking from most earthquakes can be felt for several seconds while a few can be felt for several minutes.
- Most earthquakes occur about 10 miles below the Earth's surface. They can occur as deep as 400 miles below the surface.
- An earthquake under the ocean can cause a tsunami, a catastrophic series of ocean waves often created by an undersea earthquake, which travel outward in all directions at 500 miles per hour. When the tsunami reaches the shoreline, it can roll up to heights of over 100 feet, causing massive destruction.
- The strongest earthquake ever recorded in the world was in Chile in 1960. It measured 9.6 on the Richter Scale.
- Alaska averages 24,000 earthquakes a year, the most seismic activity in North America. On March 28, 1964, a magnitude 9.2 quake occurred with shaking that lasted more than 4 minutes, and killed 131 people.
- The deadliest known earthquake occurred in China in 1556. It killed about 830,000 people.
- Parkfield, California, known as "The Earthquake Capital of the World," has a bridge that spans two tectonic plates.
- The San Andreas Fault, a famous fault in California, marks the boundary between two tectonic plates that slowly slide past each other. Because of continuously moving plates,

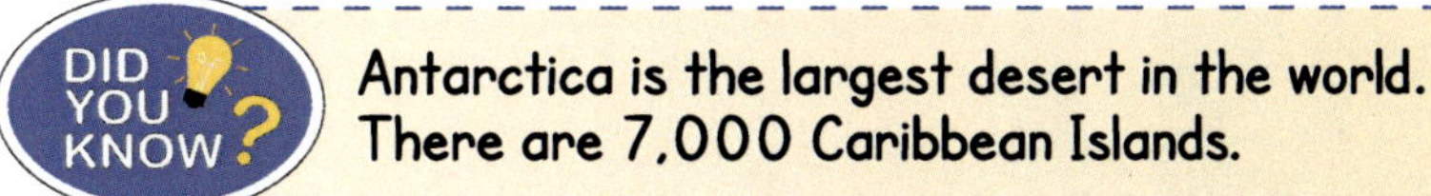

geologists predict that Los Angeles (on the Pacific Tectonic Plate) will eventually slide up next to Alaska (on the North American Plate) ... in 70 million years! (It could be neighbors with San Francisco in 15 million years.)

VOLCANOES — EARTH'S PRESSURE COOKER

The Earth has three main layers:

- The **crust** is the rocky outer layer of the Earth. It is the part on which we live and is between 20 and 60 miles thick.
- The **mantle**, the Earth's second layer, is about 1,800 miles thick.
- The **core,** the inner layer of the Earth, is about 2,100 miles thick.

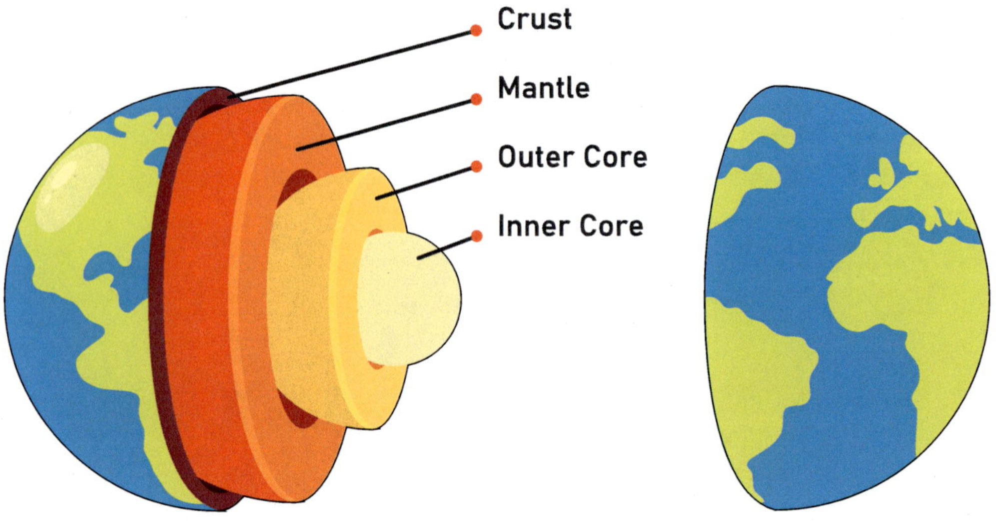

The Earth's crust is made up of huge slabs called tectonic plates, which fit together like a jigsaw puzzle. These plates are always moving. The friction causes earthquakes and volcanic eruptions near the edges of the plates. The theory that explains this process is called **plate tectonics**.

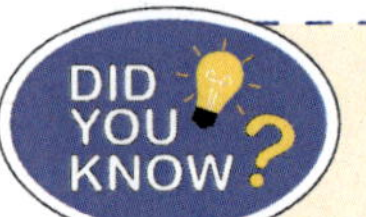

Mount Chimborazo in Ecuador is the highest point on Earth, but not the world's tallest mountain.

Volcanoes are giant safety valves that release the pressure that builds up inside the Earth. A **volcano** is a mountain opening downward to a pool of molten rock, or **magma,** below the surface of the Earth. As pressure in the molten rock builds up, it needs to escape somewhere. So, it forces its way up through **fissures,** which are narrow cracks in the Earth's crust. Once the magma erupts through the Earth's surface, it's called **lava**.

Volcanic eruptions have been known to knock down entire forests. An erupting volcano can trigger tsunamis, flash floods, earthquakes, mudflows and rockfalls, and can explode immense amounts of volcanic ash into the atmosphere, which may cause climate change around the world!

Scientists have divided volcanoes into three main categories: active, dormant, and extinct.

- An **active** volcano is one that has recently erupted and there is a possibility that it may erupt again soon.
- A **dormant** volcano is one that has not erupted in a long time (in the last 10,000 years) but there is a possibility it may erupt in the future.
- An **extinct** volcano is one that erupted thousands of years ago and is not expected to erupt again. However, occasionally extinct volcanoes do unexpectedly become active.

- The word volcano has its origin from the name of **Vulcan**, the god of fire in Roman mythology.
- There are around 1,510 active volcanoes in the world.
- Fresh lava ranges from 1,300^{0} to 2,200^{0} F. It glows red hot to white hot as it flows.
- Volcanoes have played an important role in shaping our Earth. Ash from volcanoes adds minerals to soil, which help plants grow strong. Healthy plants produce oxygen for humans and animals to breathe.
- Scientists are turning to volcanoes to help power cities. Researchers are exploring **geothermal energy,** which involves tapping into the heat beneath the Earth's surface to generate electricity. In Iceland, 25% of the nation's energy is geothermal.

- Over 70% of all Earth's volcanoes are found underwater on the ocean floor. These volcanoes form where tectonic plates pull apart from each other and create **mid-ocean ridges**, long volcanic mountain chains.
- About 75% of the Earth's land volcanoes are located in a region called the **Ring of Fire**. The ring sits along the boundaries or edges of several tectonic plates. This 25,000-mile ring is located around the Pacific Ocean. It runs from the southern tip of South America up the west coast of North America. It continues across the Bering Strait and then south through Japan to New Zealand.

CONTINENTS — A REALLY "BIG" DEAL

A **continent** is a large solid area of land. Earth has seven continents. From largest to smallest, they are Asia, Africa, North America, South America, Antarctica, Europe, and Australia.

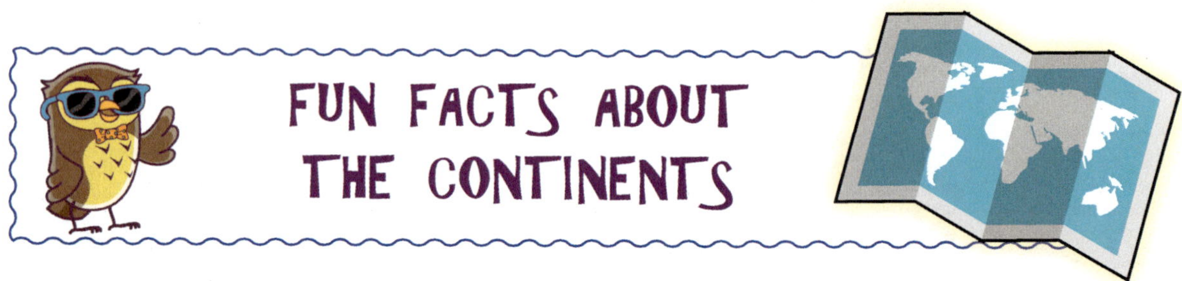

ASIA:

- Asia, the largest continent, covers one-third of Earth's surface.
- More than half the world's population, 3.2 billion people, live in Asia.
- The Earth's two most populous countries, China and India, are located in Asia.
- Asia is the birthplace of three of the world's great religions: Buddhism, Hinduism, and Islam.
- The world's biggest cave can be found in Asia.
- Asia is home to The Great Wall of China, over 5,500 miles long.
- Lake Baikal, the world's largest freshwater lake in terms of volume is situated in Asia. The lake contains about 20% of Earth's fresh surface water; that's equivalent to all five North American Great Lakes combined.

- The saltwater Caspian Sea in Asia has the greatest surface area of any lake, 143,200 square miles.
- There are 55 countries in Asia.
- The highest elevation on Earth is at the top of Mount Everest, 29,035 feet above sea.

AFRICA:

- Africa is the second largest continent.
- It is home to the Nile, the longest river in the world.
- The largest desert in the world, the Sahara, is situated in Africa.
- There are 54 countries in Africa.
- Africa used to be called "the Dark Continent" because Europe did not know much about Africa until the 19th century. They called it the Dark Continent, because of the mysteries and the savagery they expected to find in the interior.
- Scientists believe Africa to be the place where the first human beings lived.
- The equator passes through the middle of Africa.
- The world's hottest place, Ethiopia, is a country in Africa.
- Ninety-five percent of the world's diamonds come from Africa.
- More than 50% of the world's gold comes from Africa.

NORTH AMERICA:

- North America is the only continent that has every kind of climate — tropical, dry, continental, moderate, and polar.
- There are five time zones in North America.
- Lake Superior, on the United States/Canada border, is the freshwater lake with the greatest surface area in the world (31,700 square miles).

SOUTH AMERICA:

- The Andes Mountains in South America form the second highest mountain system on Earth next to the Himalayas.
- Mount Aconcagua (22,841 feet) is the Andes' highest peak.

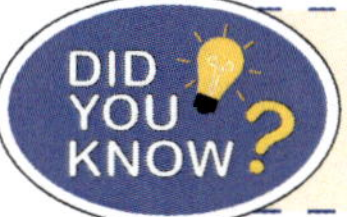

Deepest Gorge: Hells Canyon, Snake River, Idaho, 7,900 feet deep.

- The highest waterfall in the world, Angel Falls, can be found in South America.
- South America is home to the largest river by water volume, the Amazon River.
- South America is home to the anaconda, one of Earth's largest snakes.
- Both of the world's highest land volcanoes, Mount Chimborazo and Mount Cotopaxi, are found in South America.
- The world's highest lake, Lake Titicaca, 12,467 feet above sea level, is located in South America.
- Brazil, a country in South America, is the largest producer of coffee in the world.
- The primary language spoken in 13 of the 14 countries in South America is Spanish.
- Portuguese is the primary language spoken in Brazil, South America's largest and most populous nation.

ANTARCTICA:

- During the winter months, Antarctica nearly doubles in size due to the large amount of sea ice that forms along its periphery.
- Antarctica is the driest, windiest, emptiest, coldest place on Earth.
- Antarctica, which is 98% covered in ice, contains nearly 75% of the ice on Earth.
- It is estimated that ice is as much as 2½ miles thick in parts of Antarctica.
- Antarctica contains about 70% of the world's fresh water in the form of ice.
- The animals most associated with Antarctica are the Adélie and Emperor penguins.
- The water around Antarctica is so cold that nothing can rot there.
- There are miles and miles of lakes under the ice of Antarctica that have never been touched.
- The coldest temperature ever recorded on Earth was in Antarctica at –129°F *Brrrrrrr!*

EUROPE:

- Europe is the only continent that does not have any deserts.
- There are 44 countries in Europe.
- Vatican City, home of the Pope and the world's smallest country, is in Europe.
- Most countries in Europe use a single currency called the euro.
- Germany is Europe's most populous country.
- London and Paris are Europe's most populous cities.
- Russia is the largest country by area in Europe.

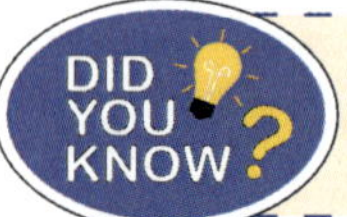

90% of the total volcanoes on the Earth are found in the horseshoe-shaped area in the Pacific Ocean called the "Ring of Fire."

AUSTRALIA:

- The name Australia comes from the Latin word *Australis,* which means "Southern."
- Australia, sometimes known as an "Island Continent," is the smallest continent in the world, covering only 3 million square miles, compared with Asia's 17.2 million square miles.
- Australia has only one country, Australia, also called "The Land Down Under."
- Two-thirds of Australia is flat desert.
- Australia's Great Barrier Reef is the world's largest coral reef.
- Australia has 14 times as many sheep as people.
- Australia ranks first in wool production and export in the world.

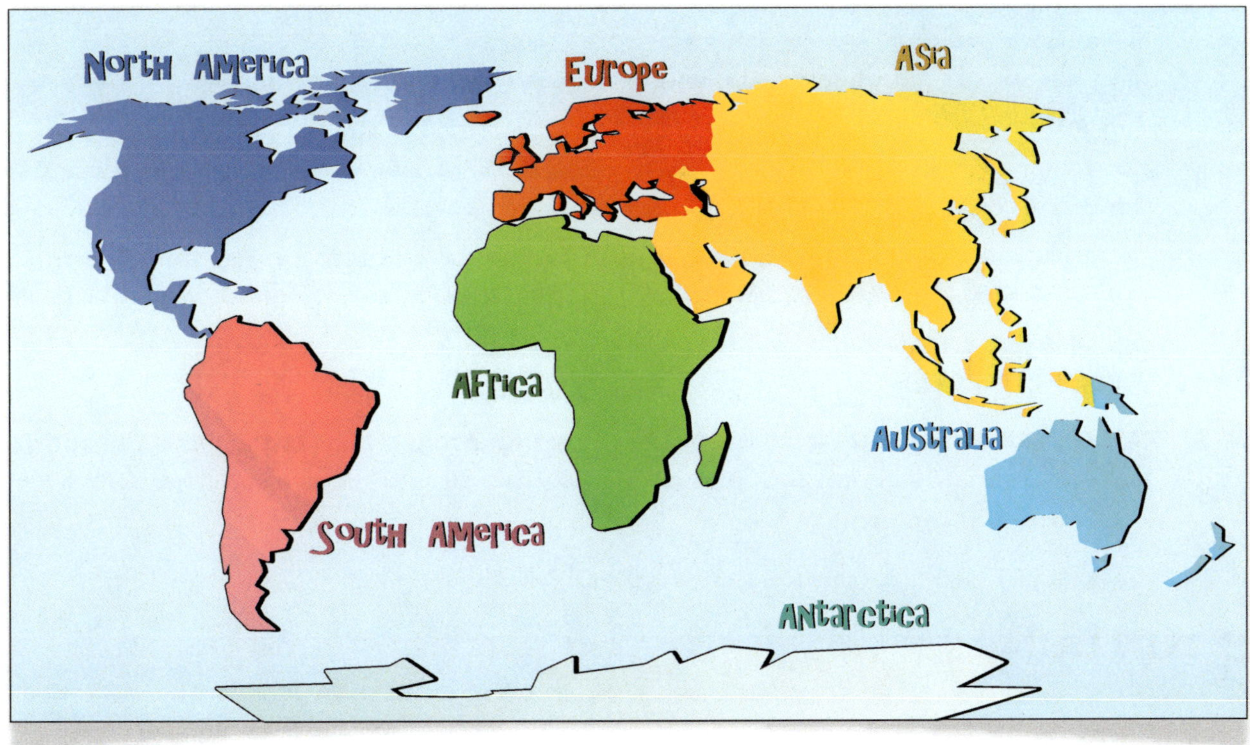

DID YOU KNOW?

Longest Mountain Range: The Andes of South America, 5,000 miles
With 317,52 lakes, Canada has more lakes than anywhere else in the world.

ISLANDS

Islands are areas of land that are completely surrounded by water. Small islands are sometimes called cays, keys, or islets. Islands are found in oceans, lakes, and rivers. A group of islands located close together is often called an **archipelago**.

FUN FACTS ABOUT ISLANDS

- Java, the world's most populated island, is home to over 130 million people.
- Greenland is the world's largest island. (Australia, which is larger, and like Greenland, is surrounded by water and is classified as a continent because of the way in which it was formed — on its own tectonic plate!)
- Great Britain, the largest island in the British Isles, is the ninth largest island in the world.
- The term "desert island" means an island with no people on it. This does not mean that the island is a desert, but rather that it is deserted.
- Around 1 in 6 people on the planet live on an island.
- Madagascar is the fourth largest island in the world. Around 80% of the plant and animal life on this island can only be found on Madagascar. It is so unique some scientists refer to it as the eighth continent.

MOUNTAINS

A **mountain** is a landform that rises 1,000 feet or more above the level of the surrounding land. Those less than 1,000 feet higher are called **hills**.

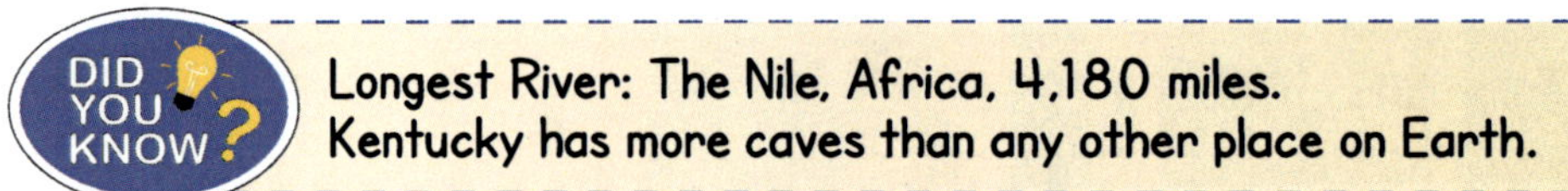

Mountains are most often formed as tectonic plates push against each other, forcing the adjoining land up. Great mountain ranges like the Himalayas often form along the boundaries of these plates. The top of a mountain is called the **summit**; the side is called the **slope**, and the steep valley between young mountains is known as a **gorge** or **canyon.**

- More than half of the world's fresh water flows from mountains.
- All of the world's major rivers are fed from mountain sources.
- Mountains cover one-fifth of the Earth's land surface and occur in 75 percent of the world's countries.
- Some of the world's highest mountains are at the bottom of the sea. The "big island" of Hawaii is at the top of Mauna Kea, a volcanic mountain in the Pacific Ocean. It is the tallest mountain from base to peak at more than 33,500 feet, but 19,700 feet of its height is submerged below the Pacific Ocean.
- The highest mountain in the world measured from the Earth's surface is Mount Everest in the Himalayas, at 29,035 feet above sea level.
- The largest range of mountains is in the Atlantic Ocean.
- A mountain may be home to many different biomes including temperate forest, taiga forest, tundra, and grassland.
- A mountain's elevation over 26,000 feet above sea level is called the "death zone" because there isn't enough oxygen to support human life.

RIVERS —THEY JUST KEEP ROLLING ALONG

A **river** is a flowing, moving stream of water -that usually feeds into an ocean, lake, pond, or even another river, and is considered part of the freshwater biome. Rivers can vary in size. The shortest river in the world, the Roe River in Montana, is only 201 feet long, while the world's longest river, the Nile, runs for 4,132 miles!

All rivers start at the highest point in an area, called their **source**, usually in mountains or hills, where rain water or melting snow collects and forms tiny streams. As a river flows downstream, it gains more water from other streams, rivers, or springs, called **tributaries**, as well as added rainfall, and other water sources. Rivers flow in **channels**. The bottom of the channel is called the **bed** and the sides of the channel are called the **banks.**

As super-powerful forces of nature, rivers carve out most of Earth's landforms — from wide, vast river valleys to plains, gorges, and even spectacular formations like the Grand Canyon in the western United States — shaping the land as they flow to the ocean. Fast-flowing rivers carry pebbles, sand, and silt. As the river begins to slow down — as in a wetland, at the outside of a bend, or where the river widens, such as at the mouth — these sediments sink and build up to form **deltas**. Rivers that overflow their banks also deposit sediment in the surrounding flood plain. These deltas and floodplains are highly fertile agricultural zones that offer tremendous value to the surrounding people. In Egypt, for example, the Nile River and its adjacent delta helped give rise to the Egyptian empire that built the pyramids. Today, farmers in the flood plain of California's Central Valley produce one-third of the vegetables and two-thirds of the fruits and nuts consumed in the United States. As necessary as rivers are, when they overrun their banks, they create floods, which cause massive destructive forces.

Sadly, our rivers and waterways are being polluted by chemicals, sewage, and household waste, which can cause serious harm to animals and humans, too. In fact, scientists estimate that 300-400 million tons of waste pollute our rivers and seas every year!

Although rivers hold only a small amount of -Earth's water, they have always been vital to every form of life on the planet.

- Rivers give water for drinking, bathing and washing clothes.
- Rivers give water for cattle and other animals to drink and for people to grow plants, including vegetables, grains, fruits, and flowers.
- Rivers give products that are useful to people such as fish for food, clay for bricks, and reeds to make rooftops for houses.
- Rivers can be used for transporting people, crops, and other goods by boat.
- Rivers can be used to give power to turn machinery such as water mills.
- Rivers give water to factories that make cloth, steel, and many other products.

- Rivers sometimes have dams to hold water for people to drink, or to make electricity.
- Rivers can be used for leisure and sports such as swimming, boating, fishing, and -simply walking by the river.

FUN FACTS ABOUT RIVERS

- The Nile River, the world's longest river, flows through 11 different countries in Africa.
- The Amazon River, the world's largest river by volume, contains 20% of the world's freshwater. It runs through the mountains and rainforests of South America.
- The world's deepest river, the Congo River in central Africa, is 720 feet deep in some parts — so deep that light cannot penetrate from the surface to the bottom.
- The Danube River flows through 10 different countries in Europe. Only the Nile flows through more countries.Not all rivers flow overland — subterranean rivers run secretly beneath the surface. This is sometimes because of human engineering and sometimes because of nature. London's "lost rivers" are streams of the River Thames and River Lea that were built over as the city grew. Subterranean rivers can also exist naturally. In the Philippines, the Puerto Princesa flows *beneath* a mountain for five miles before finally emptying into the South China Sea.
- Rivers change over time. Floods may make them larger, and droughts cause them to shrink or dry up. People and animals change them too. People build dams, as do beavers.
- Rivers provide a home for all kinds of creatures, including insects, amphibians, birds, reptiles, mammals, and over 10,000 species of fish!
- Rivers and lakes are a vital source of freshwater for life on Earth, but they hold *less than 1%* of the world's water. Over 99% of Earth's water is in the salty ocean and frozen in our polar ice caps.
- There are 76 rivers in the world over 1,000 miles long.
- Many people think rivers always flow south, but 4 of the 10 longest rivers in the world flow north.
- The United States has around 3.5 million miles of rivers.
- Four of the 10 longest rivers flow through Russia at some point, and four of the 10 longest rivers flow through China at some point as well.

OCEANS AND SEAS

While **oceans** are large bodies of water unobstructed by continents, **seas** can be any body of salt water. A sea usually refers to a body of salt water partially or completely enclosed by land. The oceans and seas of the world are actually one big ocean because they are all connected.

The five world oceans in order from largest to smallest are the Pacific, the Atlantic, the Indian, the Southern (Antarctic), and the Arctic. The five largest seas in order from largest to smallest are the South China Sea, the Caribbean, the Mediterranean, the Bering, and the Gulf of Mexico.

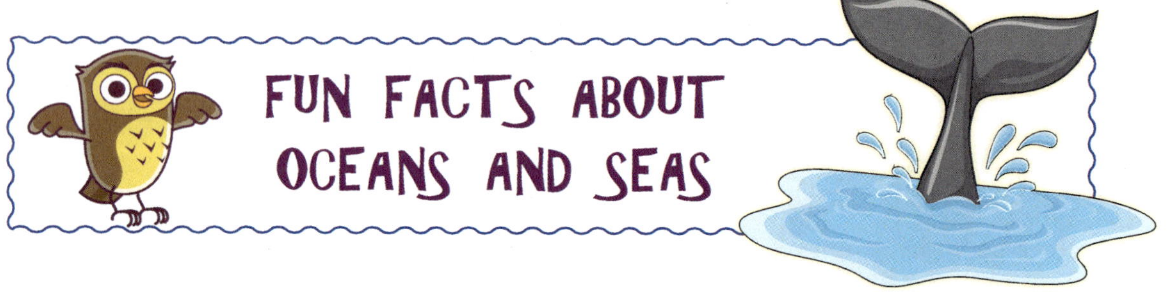

- Oceans form the Earth's largest ecosystem, covering over 70 percent of the surface of the planet. Without the oceans, life on Earth would not be possible.
- Because of its huge surface area, enormous quantities of water evaporate from the oceans and seas into the atmosphere where they condense into clouds and fall as rain. This water cycle is critical to life on Earth.
- The sun warms the ocean and sea waters. The heat from the water warms the atmosphere, which helps keep the Earth warm and livable. Without this heat, Earth would be very cold.
- The oceans have absorbed almost 90% of the additional heat created by human activities over the last 50 years, which significantly helped keep our atmosphere cooler than it would otherwise be.
- The underwater landscape of the ocean is as varied in structure and appearance as that on land. There are huge mountains, deep canyons, and vast plains.

OCEAN CURRENTS — U-HAULS OF THE OCEANS

In 1992, a cargo ship carrying bath toys got caught in a storm. Shipping containers washed overboard, and the waves swept 28,000 rubber ducks and other toys into the North Pacific. But they didn't stick together — the ducks have since washed up all over the world. These ducks and their worldwide adventure unexpectedly helped researchers chart how ocean currents work.

An **ocean current** is a continuous movement of ocean water from one place to another. Ocean currents are created by wind, water temperature, salt content, and the gravity of the moon. The current's direction and speed depend on the shoreline and the ocean floor. They can flow for thousands of miles and are found in all the oceans of the world. Ocean currents can be found on the water surface and deeper down. One major example of an ocean current is the **Gulf Stream** in the Atlantic Ocean.

THE GULF STREAM

Imagine that you are at a water park containing one of those wonderful lazy rivers. When you first look at that river, it looks so relaxing to just take an inner tube and float on the water. You notice how everyone is floating in the same direction. You realize that when you put your foot in the water, you can feel the water flowing past you in the same direction everyone is floating. If you were to try to walk against this flow of water, it would be very hard. What you are experiencing is a **current** of water, or water moving in a certain direction.

The Gulf Stream is a strong, warm ocean current that starts in the Gulf of Mexico and flows around the tip of Florida, into the Atlantic Ocean, and north along the eastern coast of the United States. The water in the Gulf Stream flows very quickly (300 times faster than the Amazon River!) and moves more water than all of the world's rivers combined. As the water moves along the path of the Gulf Stream, it brings the heat and warm air from the south to the north.

The waters in the Gulf of Mexico tend to be pretty warm, usually about 80^{0} F. As the Gulf Stream pushes the warm water through its path, it helps to take warmer air not only up and along the eastern coast of the United States, but all the way across the ocean to the northwestern parts of Europe. The Gulf Stream is an example of how a current can have a profound impact on climate. It pulls warm water from the equator to the coast of Western Europe. As a result, areas such as the United Kingdom are typically much warmer than areas at the same northern latitude in North America.

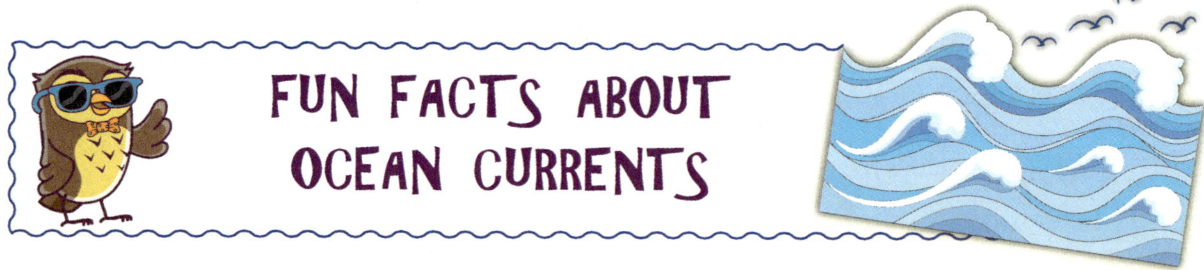

- Surface currents are important to ships, as they can make it easy or difficult to travel depending on the direction of the current.
- Some marine animals take advantage of currents to migrate thousands of miles to and from breeding grounds.
- The first mention of the Gulf Stream (before it even had a name) was in the records of Ponce de Leon, an explorer who, in 1513, mentioned running into a current that was more powerful than the wind.
- In 1770, Ben Franklin published the first map and gave the Gulf Stream its name.

BIOMES — WHERE IS MY HOME?

A **biome**, also called a **habitat**, is an area of the planet that is classified according to the plants and animals that live in it. Temperature, soil, and the amount of light and water help determine what life exists in a biome. A biome is different from an **ecosystem.** An ecosystem is the interaction of living and nonliving things in an environment. A biome is a specific geographic area notable for the species living there. A biome can be made up of many ecosystems. For example, an aquatic biome can contain ecosystems such as coral reefs and kelp forests.

Biomes move as the climate changes. Ten thousand years ago, parts of north Africa were lush landscapes cut by flowing rivers. Gradually, the climate dried out. Today, this region is part of the world's largest desert, the Sahara.

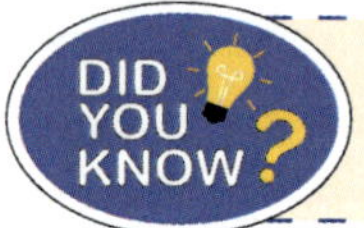

Continents shift at about the same rate as our fingernails grow.

Forest Biomes

All forests have lots of trees, but there are different types of forests. They are often described as different biomes. One of the main differences is where they are located in relation to the equator and the poles. There are three main types of forest biomes: the tropical rainforest, the temperate forest, and the taiga. **Tropical rainforests** are located in the tropics, near the equator. **Taiga forests** are located far north. **Temperate rainforests** are located in between in several locations around the world, usually halfway between the equator and the poles.

WHAT MAKES A FOREST A TEMPERATE FOREST?

- **Temperature:** Temperate means "not too extreme" or "in moderation." It never gets really hot (like in the tropical rainforest) or really cold (like in the taiga) here. The temperature is generally between minus 20^0 F. and 90^0 F.
- **Four seasons:** There are four distinct seasons: winter, spring, summer, and fall. Each season is about the same length of time. With only a three-month winter, plants have a long growing season.
- **Lots of rain**: There is usually between 30 and 60 inches of rain per year.
- **Fertile soil**: Rotted leaves and other decaying matter provide a rich, deep soil that is good for trees to grow strong roots.

WHAT MAKES A FOREST A TAIGA FOREST?

The taiga has several characteristics that distinguish it from the other forest biomes:

- **Evergreen trees:** This forest is covered with evergreen or coniferous trees, which are trees that don't drop their leaves or needles in the winter. They keep their leaves so they can soak up as much sunlight for as long as possible. The dark green color of their leaves helps them use more sunlight and gain more energy through photosynthesis, the process by which green plants and some other organisms use sunlight to synthesize foods from carbon dioxide and water.
- **Cold weather:** The taiga has the coldest weather of the forest biomes. Winters can get as cold as -60^0 F. Winter can last for six months with the temperature averaging below freezing. Summers are warmer, but very short.
- **Dry:** The precipitation is only slightly more than the desert or the tundra. Average precipitation is between 12 and 30 inches per year.

- **Thin layer of soil:** Because the leaves don't fall from the trees, as in the temperate forest, the layer of soil is thin. Also, the cold weather causes a slow rate of decay, which takes it longer for nutrients to get back into the soil.
- **Short growing season:** With a long winter and short summer, plants don't have a lot of time with sunlight to grow in the taiga. The growing season only lasts for around three months, compared to six months in the temperate forest and a year-round growing season in the tropical rainforest.
- The largest taiga forest covers much of northern Russia and Siberia. Other major taiga forests can be found in Canada, Alaska, Finland, Norway, and Sweden.

WHAT MAKES A FOREST A TROPICAL RAINFOREST?

One of the most fascinating biomes on planet Earth is the tropical rainforest. It is filled with tall trees, interesting plants, giant insects, and all sorts of animals.

- **Rain:** As you might have guessed from the name, rainforests are forests that get a lot of rain — about 75 to 100 inches a year.
- **In the tropics:** Located near the equator, between the Tropic of Cancer and the Tropic of Capricorn.
- **Very humid and warm:** Because they are close to the equator, the temperature in tropical rainforests stays between 70° F. and 90° F. for most of the year.
- **Biodiversity:** The tropical rainforest has the most biodiversity of all the land biomes. Despite only covering around 6% of the Earth's surface, scientists estimate that half of the planet's animal and plant species live in the world's tropical rainforests.
- **Three main layers:** The rainforest can be divided into three main layers: the canopy, the understory, and the forest floor. Different animals and plants live in each layer.
    - ◊ **The canopy:** This is the top layer of trees. These trees are usually at least 100 feet tall. Their branches and leaves form an umbrella over the rest of the layers. Many of the plants and animals live in this layer. This layer includes monkeys, birds, insects, and reptiles of all sorts. Some animals can live their entire lives without leaving the canopy to touch the ground. This layer is the loudest layer with the animals making lots of noise.

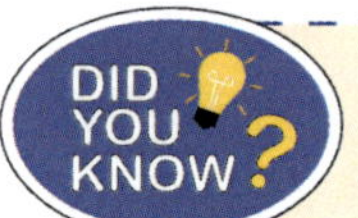

The Dead Sea, the lowest point on land, is currently 1385 feet below sea level and sinking about 3 feet a year.

◊ **The understory:** Beneath the canopy is the understory. It's made up of some shorter trees and shrubs, but mostly the trunks and branches of the canopy trees. This layer is home to larger predators like snakes and leopards, as well as owls, bats, insects, frogs, and iguanas.

◊ **The forest floor:** Because of the thickness of the canopy, very little sunlight makes it to the forest floor. This layer is home to insects, spiders, deer, pigs, and snakes. This layer is the quietest layer as animals sneak around in the dark making little noise.

Unfortunately, human development is killing off much of the world's tropical rainforests. Around 40% of the world's rainforests have already been lost. Environmentalists are doing what they can to help countries preserve this vital biome.

- Surprisingly, the soil in a rainforest is shallow, poor, and has few nutrients.
- In the Amazon rainforest, there are over 2,000 species of butterflies.
- Tropical rainforests are home to interesting "flying" animals such as squirrels, snakes, and frogs. These animals do not truly fly; rather, they glide between trees.
- It is estimated that 25% of the ingredients in medicines today come from the tropical rainforest.
- Tropical rainforests impact the temperatures and weather patterns throughout the world.
- Nearly one-fifth of the world's freshwater supply is in the Amazon rainforest.
- A section of rainforest the size of a football field is cut down every second.
- Only about 2% of the sunlight hits the forest floor in the tropical rainforest.

Grassland Biomes

Grasslands are wide expanses of land filled with low-growing plants such as grasses and wildflowers. The amount of rain is not enough to grow tall trees and produce a forest, but it is enough to avoid the formation of a desert. The temperate grasslands have seasons including a hot summer and a cold winter. Grasslands are generally located between deserts and forests. The grassland biome plays an important role in human farming and food. This biome is used to grow staple crops such as wheat and corn, and is also good for grazing livestock such as cattle.

Each major area of grasslands in the world has its own characteristics and is often called by other names:

Prairie: Grasslands in North America are called the prairies. They cover around 1.4 million square miles of the central United States, southern Canada, and northern Mexico. Only around 2% of the original prairies of North America still exist in their natural state. Much of it has been turned into farmland.

Steppes: The steppes are grasslands that cover eastern Hungary, Ukraine, and southern Russia all the way to Mongolia. The steppes stretch over 4,000 miles of Asia including much of the fabled Silk Road from China to Europe.

Pampas: The grasslands in South America, called the pampas, cover around 300,000 square miles between the Andes Mountains and the Atlantic Ocean.

Conservation efforts are going on to try and save the grasslands that are left, as well as the endangered plants and animals that call the grasslands home.

Tundra Biome

The **tundra** is a treeless plain or barren land. It is a cold, harsh place, which makes it hard for plants and animals to survive. Around 20% of the Earth's land surface is covered by tundra. Characteristics of the tundra include:

- **Cold:** The tundra is the coldest of the biomes. The average temperature in the tundra is around -18^{0} F. It gets much colder in the winter and only somewhat warmer during its short summer.
- **Dry:** The tundra gets about as much precipitation as the average desert, around 10 inches per year. Most of this precipitation is in the form of snow.
- **Barren:** The tundra has few nutrients to support plant and animal life. It has a short growing season and a slow rate of decay.
- **Permafrost:** Below the topsoil, the ground is permanently frozen year-round.

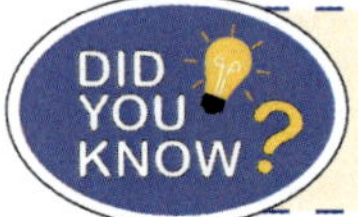

California has more people than all of Canada. Canada: 37.74 million. California: 39.78 million. (According to data from 2020.)

FUN FACTS ABOUT THE TUNDRA

- The tundra is a very fragile biome that is shrinking as the permafrost melts.
- Lemmings are small mammals that live in the tundra biome and burrow under the snow to eat grasses and moss during the winter. Polar bears come to the tundra for the summer to give birth to their cubs.
- Animals in the tundra tend to have small ears and tails, which help them stay warmer in the cold. They have large feet, which help them to walk on top of the snow.
- Plants that grow in tight groups to protect themselves from the cold are sometimes called cushion plants.
- The Inuit people of Alaska live on the tundra.

Desert Biome

Deserts are primarily defined by lack of rain. They generally get less than 10 inches of rain in a year. Deserts have dry, rich soil, little or no surface water, and high evaporation. Sometimes rain evaporates before it can hit the ground!

The largest hot and dry desert in the world is the Sahara Desert in northern Africa. This sandy desert with giant sand dunes covers over 3 million square miles. Other major deserts include the Arabian Desert in the Middle East, the Gobi Desert in northern China and Mongolia, and the Kalahari Desert in southern Africa.

Animals that live in the desert have adapted to needing little water. Many get all the water they need from the food they eat. Other animals store water that they can use later.

FUN FACTS ABOUT THE DESERT

- The camel stores fat, not water, in its hump while other animals store reserves in their tails. Camels can go without water for a week. A thirsty camel can drink 30 gallons of water in less than 15 minutes.

- Only certain types of plants can survive the harsh environment of the desert. These include cacti, grasses, shrubs, and some short trees. You won't see a lot of tall trees in the desert. Most desert plants have a way to store water in their stems, leaves, or trunks so they can survive a long time without water. They tend to be spread out from each other and have a large root system so they can gather up all the water possible when it does rain.
- Many desert plants are armed with sharp spines and needles to help protect them from animals.
- The giant saguaro cactus can grow 50 feet tall and live for 200 years.
- Plants that store water in their stems are called **succulents**. Some desert trees have taproots that go 30 feet deep to find water.
- Currently, deserts cover around 20% of the world's land, but they are growing. This is called **desertification** and is caused by different factors, including human activities. The Sahara Desert is expanding at the rate of around 30 miles per year.
- Because the desert is so dry, the wind will grind pebbles and sand into dust. Occasionally, the wind will gather up this dust into a huge storm. Dust storms can be over 1 mile high and so thick with dust that you can't breathe. They can travel for over a thousand miles.
- Dust storms from the Gobi Desert have been known to reach Beijing, China, nearly 1,000 miles away.
- Because they are not extensively farmed and minerals that have not been used are embedded in the ground, deserts have some of the richest soil on Earth. All deserts need is sufficient water to cause almost every kind of plant to grow here.
- Not every desert is hot. Some of them are among the coldest places on Earth.
- Antarctica is the coldest, windiest, and most isolated continent on Earth, and is considered a desert because its annual precipitation can be less than 2 inches in the interior.

Aquatic Biomes

There are two major aquatic or water biomes, the **marine biome** and the **freshwater biome**.

MARINE BIOME

The marine biome is primarily made up of saltwater, and can be divided into three types:

- **Oceans:** As stated earlier, there are five major oceans that cover the world.
- **Coral reefs:** Coral reefs are small in size when compared to the oceans, but around 25% of marine species live in the coral reefs, which makes them an important biome.

- **Estuaries:** Estuaries are areas where freshwater rivers and streams flow into the salty ocean. This combination of freshwater and seawater, known as brackish water, creates an ecosystem or biome with interesting and diverse plant and animal life.
- The marine biome, which covers about 70% of the Earth's surface, is the largest biome and has the greatest biodiversity of all the biomes on Earth. Thousands of species of animals and plants live in the ocean. They rely on photosynthesis from the sun for energy. Plants in the ocean are extremely important to all life on planet Earth. Algae in the ocean absorbs carbon dioxide and provides much of the Earth's oxygen. Examples of algae include kelp and phytoplankton. Other ocean plants are seaweeds, sea grasses, and mangroves.

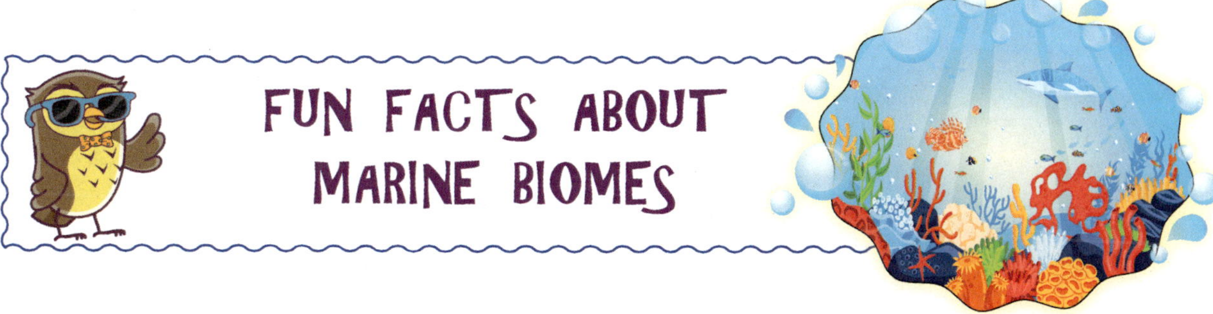

- Over 90% of the life on Earth lives in the ocean.
- The average depth of the ocean is 12,400 feet.
- Over 70% of all volcanic activity takes place in the world's oceans.
- The **Mariana Trench,** the deepest point in the ocean, is 36,000 feet deep.
- The largest animal on Earth, the blue whale, lives in the ocean.
- Humans get most of their protein by eating fish from the ocean.
- The average temperature of the ocean is around 39^{0} F.

FRESHWATER BIOME

The **freshwater biome** has a low salt content as opposed to the saltwater marine biome. There are three main types of freshwater biomes: **ponds and lakes, streams and rivers**, and **wetlands.**

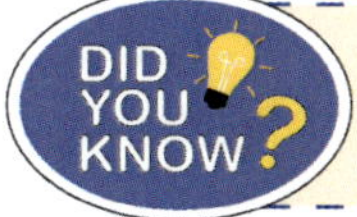

Originally built on a lake in 1325, Mexico City is currently sinking by about 3.2 feet per year.

Lakes are large bodies of water that are surrounded by land and are not part of an ocean.

- Lakes are relatively still bodies of water when compared to rivers, where water flows. They can contain either salt or freshwater and are larger than ponds.
- Lakes can form in different ways such as in the craters of volcanoes, by sinkholes in the ground, or even artificially by dams made by humans. The largest lake by surface area in the world is the Caspian Sea, a saltwater lake.
- Some of the other larger and more important lakes in the world are the Great Lakes, Lake Baikal, Lake Tanganyika, Lake Victoria, and Lake Titicaca.

Rivers and streams have flowing waters, unlike the stiller waters of ponds and lakes. This biome can vary in size from small, trickling streams to mile-wide rivers that travel for thousands of miles.

- All rivers start at the highest point in an area. As the river flows downstream, it collects more and more water from other streams, rivers, springs, rainfall, and other sources of water. Thus, it gets bigger along the way.
- A river flows across the surface of the land, normally winding its way to the sea.
- All rivers flow in channels.
- The bottom of the channel is called the **bed**, while the sides of the river are called the **banks.**
- The end of the river is called the **mouth**, and the beginning of the river is called the **head.**
- A **watershed** is the area of land where all the streams and rivers flow together.
- The longest river in the world is the Nile River in Africa.

Wetlands — Migration Stop, Hotel, Restaurant, Nursery

Wetlands are a combination of land and water: they are "*wet lands.*" One of the key characteristics of a wetland is that it supports a combination of diverse plants, animals, and microscopic aquatic life. To constitute a wetland, an area must have three characteristics during most of the growing season: hydric (saturated) soils; water-tolerant plants; and enough water to either saturate the soil or cover the land to a shallow depth. Most wetlands with their abundance of food, vegetative cover (shelter) and water, are rich with diverse wildlife species. Coastal and inland marshes, for example, are the breeding, resting, and wintering habitats for thousands of migratory birds.

Wetlands include **bogs, swamps**, and **marshes**. They are often located near large bodies of water like lakes and rivers and can be found throughout the world.

- **Marshes** are wetlands without trees.
- **Swamps** are wetlands that grow trees and have seasonal flooding.
- **Tidal swamps** are sometimes called **mangrove swamps** because mangroves can grow in the mix of freshwater and saltwater.

FUN FACTS ABOUT WETLANDS

- Wetlands cover about 6% of the Earth's surface. They can be found in every one of the United States and on all continents except Antarctica.
- Wetlands play an important role in nature. When located near rivers, wetlands can help prevent flooding.
- They are natural filtering systems and thus they purify the environment.
- Wetlands have a huge diversity of animal and plant life. Amphibians, birds, and reptiles all do well in the wetlands.
- Wetland plants may grow entirely underwater or float on top of the water.
- Two of the largest wetlands in the United States are the Everglades (1½ million acres ranging over 7,800 square miles) in southern Florida, and the Okefenokee Swamp (438,000 acres covering 684 square miles) straddling the Georgia-Florida line.
- The largest wetland in the world is the Pantanal, which covers more than 42 million acres and sprawls across three countries in South America.

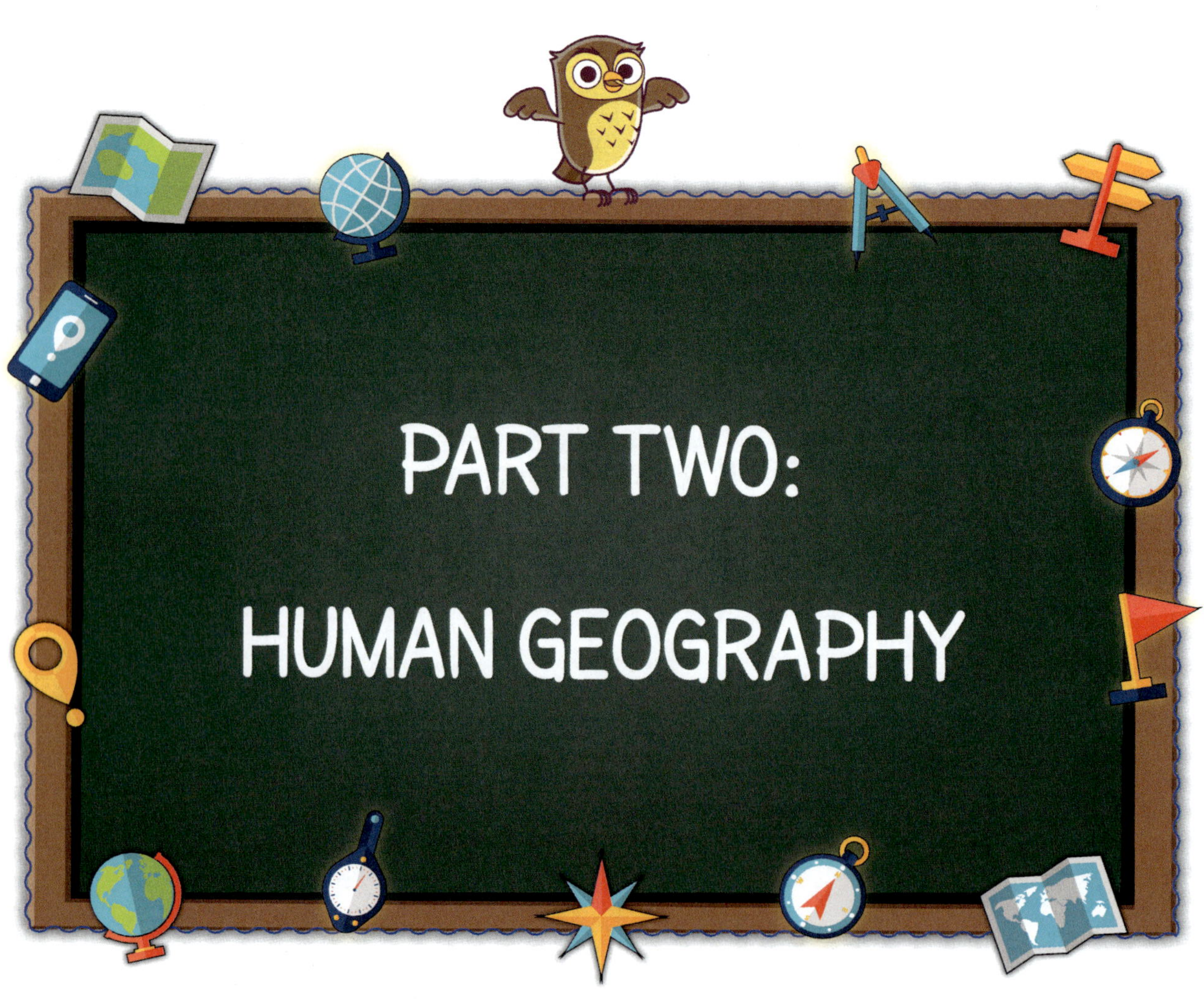

PART TWO:

HUMAN GEOGRAPHY

Humans are the only known species to have successfully populated, adapted to, and significantly altered a wide variety of land regions across the world, resulting in profound historical and environmental impacts.

The study of human geography looks at different peoples, their communities, culture and economies, how they interact with the environment around them, and how their activities affect the planet.

OUR JOURNEY BEGINS

Approximately 2.3 million years ago, early relatives of today's human beings began to make and use simple tools. By a million years ago, they had learned to control fire. ***Homo sapiens***, the first modern humans, evolved between 200,000 and 300,000 years ago. They began moving outside of Africa, and started populating parts of Europe and Asia about 70,000-100,000 years ago. Humans reached the Australian continent in canoes between 35,000 and 65,000 years ago. Scientists studying land masses and climate know that the Pleistocene Ice Age created a **land bridge** that connected Asia and North America (Alaska) over 13,000 years ago. A widely accepted migration theory is that people crossed this land bridge and eventually migrated into North and South America.

Our earliest ancestors were **hunters and gatherers**, who hunted wild animals or gathered vegetables that did not replenish themselves once they were picked. Nature never assured these human beings with a dependable source of food, so they led a **nomadic** existence, never settling in one place, but following animals and edible plants as they moved to different locations. We can't be sure why humans first migrated from the African continent, but it was likely due to the depletion of resources and the increased competition for those resources.

About 50,000 years ago, human beings developed a capacity for **language,** which allowed people to make plans, solve problems, and organize effectively. Once humans were able to communicate, they could assess whether the pressures in their current home outweighed the risk of leaving to find a new one.

THE IN-BETWEEN TIMES

When humans migrated from Africa to colder climates, they made clothing out of animal skins and constructed fires to keep themselves warm. Often, they burned fires continuously through the winter. Sophisticated weapons, such as spears and bows and arrows, allowed them to kill large mammals efficiently. Along with changing climates, these hunting methods contributed to the extinction of huge land mammals such as mammoths, giant kangaroos, and mastodons, limited the hunters' available prey.

The **Neolithic** rw (New Stone Age), which occurred between 15,000 and 7,000 years ago, marked a period when humans began to use the Earth's resources in new ways. They gradually shifted from nomadic lifestyles to fixed homes, evolving from nomadic hunting and gathering bands to settled communities. Semipermanent settlements became villages, and then towns, as people developed agricultural practices.

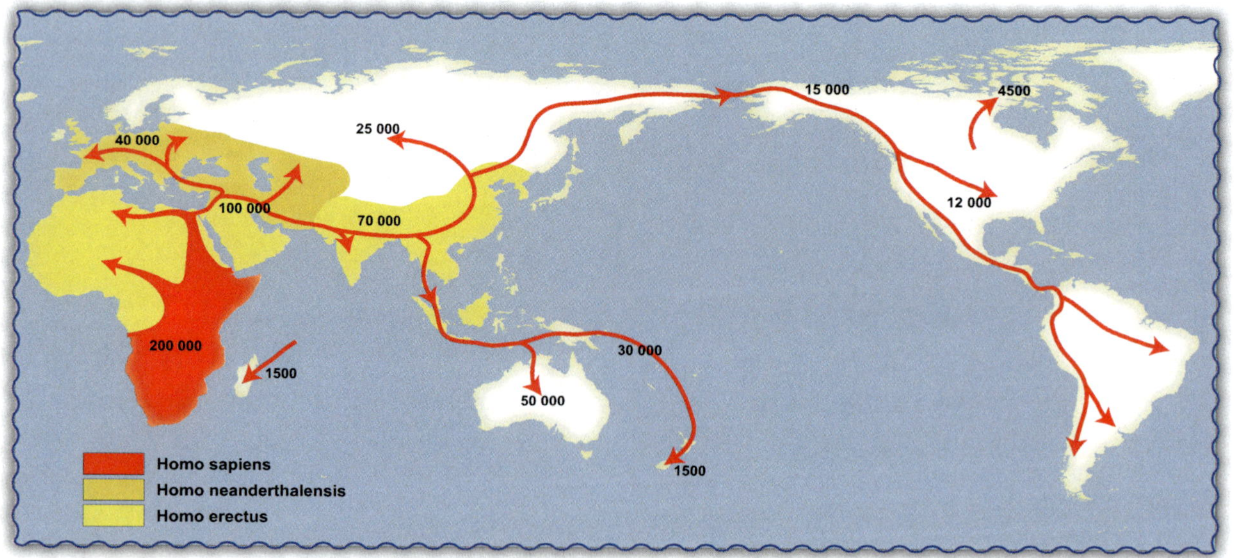

Map of the world that shows the spread of humankind throughout Earth over time. *Homo sapiens* are reflected with red arrows (shown populating the entire world over time), *Homo neanderthalensis* is reflected in orange in what is Europe and the Middle East today, and *Homo erectus* is represented in yellow in Africa, South Asia, and Southeast Asia.

AGRICULTURE AND DOMESTICATION — THE WORLD TURNED UPSIDE DOWN

The most important development in human history was the development of **agriculture**, another word for farming. It is believed that people first began farming around 12,000 years ago. Learning to farm meant learning to control wild plants — when they grow, where they grow, and selecting seeds from the best plants to make a better crop next year. This process is called **domestication**. Domestication means taking something from the wild — plant or animal — and controlling the breeding to create the type of plant or animal that is most desirable for one's needs. The ability to control wild plants and animals (food supply) is another sign of intelligence unique to human beings.

People learned to domesticate and vastly improve and enhance the usefulness of both plants and animals through observation, trial, and creative adjustments over hundreds of years. For example, when corn was a wild plant, it was the size of a human thumb. Farmers wanted bigger corn, so they saved the largest corn for next year's seed. This slowly increased the size of corn until today we have comparatively huge, delicious ears of corn.

Likewise with animals, as farming increased, people needed animals with different characteristics, both for food and to help with the work. It wasn't long before human beings learned that the same process that had worked with corn and other plants also worked to improve the utility of animals such as dogs, sheep, goats, cows, chickens, and such. By controlling the breeding, humans made cows calm, big, tastier, and more nutritious. Dogs became loyal hunters and better friends. Sheep provided more, warmer, and softer wool. Southwest Asia was the first place farming developed — mainly because that area had the highest number of plants and animals that could be domesticated.

Farming created a lifestyle that forced many changes in the lives of nomadic hunter-gatherers. Fewer people led a nomadic lifestyle because farming forced nomadic people to live in one place — to take care of and protect their fields. These new farmers usually settled along a river and created the first villages and towns. River valleys were perfect for farming, so many people settled in the same area. Water for **irrigation**, the watering of farm fields or gardens, was available from the river.

The soil near rivers is very **fertile**, full of plant food, and good for growing because most rivers regularly flooded. When an area around a river flooded, the water would soak into the ground and a thin layer of **silt,** a very fertile soil, would be left on the ground. Slowly, more people moved into these river areas. Villages grew into small towns, which, in time, evolved into the first cities around 11,000 years ago.

Farming had other effects on lifestyle and society. In hunter-gatherer tribes, nearly everyone looked for food or water throughout the whole day. Since one farmer could produce enough food for several people, other people could now experiment and discover new things in the world around them. This led to the discovery and mining of natural metals, the use of plants as medicine, the development of religious beliefs and artistic pursuits, and the need to provide for the general security of the citizens. Extra food and free time led to the development of **division of labor**, where people did different jobs, created different products, and then traded their goods or services with one another.

NEW IDEAS, NEW KNOWLEDGE, AND A NEW WAY OF LIFE

The world was rapidly changing and peoples' lives changed depending on evolving needs. As people traded and farmed, they needed a way to keep track of when to plant seeds or how much they had traded. The necessity of record keeping led to the development of a **written language**. Written languages usually started as drawings. Ideas (such as fear, joy, etc.) are hard to draw, so people made symbols to represent them. Eventually idea-symbols were replaced with sound symbols, like our alphabet. During ancient times, more than 90 percent were illiterate. As recently as 300 years ago, most people in the world still couldn't read and write.

All of these changes created a new way of life called **civilization**. A civilization is an advanced society with farming, division of labor, multiple cities, organized religion, science/technology, some form of government, and a written language. Most historians think the first four civilizations started about 3500 B.C.E. in Mesopotamia, Egypt, India, and China. The main factor that allowed civilization to develop was farming.

THE RISE OF CITIES, THE RISE OF NATIONS

Agriculture and manufacturing led to the development of marketplaces, which grew into towns, then cities. There were many considerations necessary to founding a city. Favorable land had to be located. Good sources of water and land to grow food were usually at the top of the list. It was also important to have access to navigable bodies of water so that goods could easily be transported to different areas.

Before the invention of modern warfare techniques, many cities were founded for defensive purposes. Walled cities were common in ancient history, when walls could protect a city from attack. The invention of modern heavy artillery and aerial warfare rendered the protection of walled cities useless. As populations grew, cities also became important centers of government.

CHALLENGES FOR TODAY AND TOMORROW

Pollution is anything that's introduced into the environment that has the potential to negatively influence the quality of life for humans, animals, or plants. Some types of pollution are visible or smelly, such as smoke coming from a factory, while others can't be seen or smelled at all. Similarly, some kinds of pollution affect the planet on a global scale, while the effects of others are sometimes experienced in a more localized, smaller area.

Air Pollution

There are many sources of air pollution. Cars, planes, trucks, and other vehicles that burn fossil fuels like gasoline to power their engines contribute to air pollution. If you see, smell, or breathe in the smoke that comes out of our vehicles, what you are experiencing is carbon dioxide.

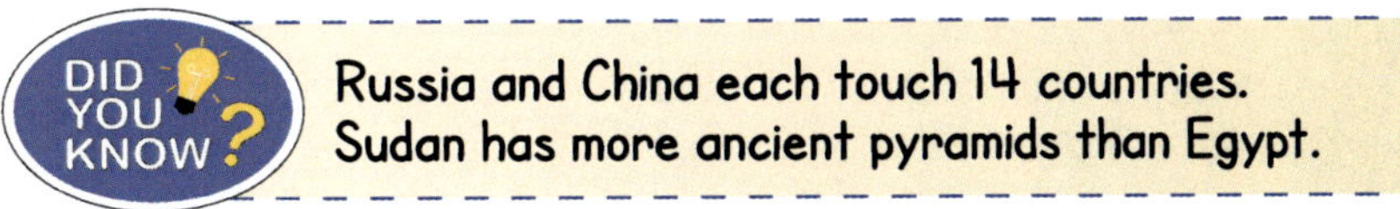

But the toxic smoke coming out of our vehicles is just a small part of our air pollution problem today. Factories that produce many of the consumer products on which we have come to depend, as well as the packaging for almost all the products we use, give off toxic substances that pollute our air.

In the section on global warming, we discussed how human activities are adding more carbon dioxide than Earth's atmosphere can absorb, thus causing our planet's temperature to rise. Although air pollution is most noticeable in urban areas, each of us experiences the negative result of human activities every day. Everything from smog to respiratory diseases such as asthma, to global warming, is caused by human-induced air pollution.

Land Pollution

Today, each of us shares our home planet with 7 billion people. Can you imagine how much trash is produced by that many human beings each day? Did you ever think about where all that trash goes?

Some of the stuff we throw away is toxic to our environment. Plastic, for example, contains chemicals that can leak into the ground and contaminate the water we drink. These chemicals, and plastics, can reach not only the land on which we live, but also oceans, rivers, and lakes.

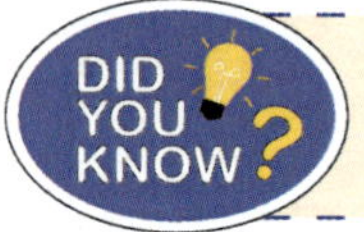

Beneath Yellowstone National Park lies an active super-volcano. Sweden has more than 267,000 islands.

We should practice the 3 Rs — Reduce, Reuse, and Recycle — by minimizing the waste that ends up in landfills so that we don't contaminate our environment. If we really need to throw out our trash, we should do so properly by bringing it to recycling centers, where the materials can be used to make other new products. This is the most effective way to manage our waste and keep this trash from reaching our landfills.

Water Pollution

What will we do when we run out of clean water to drink? What happens when the oceans, rivers, and lakes are so polluted that all the fish and aquatic animals suffer? Water, like air, is a basic essential element of life itself.

There was a time when many of us could safely drink fresh water from our faucets. But now, due to pollutants mentioned above, we don't know if our water is really safe to drink. In fact, today so many of us buy and use purified water in plastic bottles that we cause an even greater and more dangerous form of pollution: plastic pollution. But plastic is only one of several sources of water pollution.

We throw trash into oceans, lakes, and rivers, not thinking about the results it causes. Cruise ships dispose of most of their trash, including human waste, into our navigable waters, while other tankers have accidents that spill toxic oil into the ocean and cause havoc to our marine biomes. We need to stop throwing our trash into the oceans and, instead, dispose of it properly on land.

Noise Pollution

Although we hardly ever think about it, 7 billion human beings are hardly silent. Think about everything from the roar of millions of diesel trucks to the blare of hundreds of television channels, the often dissonant cheers of hundreds of thousands of people at a football game or a rock concert, to the endlessly annoying beep of horns on the freeway during traffic commute hours.

Space Pollution

As hard as it is to imagine, human beings even create "space trash." Did you ever think of how many spacecraft and artificial satellites we propel into a very small portion of outer space that surrounds Earth each year? Sure, these machines make our lives much more convenient through GPS systems, intercontinental communications, accurate weather forecasting, and even humankind's ascent to extraterrestrial bodies, but there is a cost involved.

The space around our planet has become overcrowded. Each of these billion-dollar efforts can, and sometimes do, collide with one another — and the vast assortment of space junk poses a threat to each newly launched spacecraft.

Food Pollution

Many sources of food we eat, from meat to fish to milk to vegetables, are stuffed full of man-made chemicals and compounds to make them grow larger, more tender, more tasty, and more visually attractive in the shortest amount of time possible. This is wonderfully convenient for us, but some of these additives enter our bodies and constitute pollutants. Some of them cause cancer and other diseases, and others cause us to lose part of our auto-immune system. And we still have yet to know how other additives might negatively affect our bodies

PLASTIC POLLUTION — CAN TINY PIECES OF LITTER FORM AN ISLAND?

There is one extremely widespread and pernicious form of pollution for which we've reserved a special section of its own: **plastic pollution.**

A sea otter carefully uses its paws to free itself from a plastic bag that's tangled loosely around its body. This sea otter isn't the only animal to have a dangerous run-in with litter: It's estimated that about half of all marine mammals have eaten or been trapped by plastic.

Plastic pollution is different from paper or food waste because it never fully decomposes, or breaks down into pieces that can be reused by nature. Instead, plastic often ends up in water, where it releases toxic chemicals and can be mistaken for food. In a study conducted by the journal *Science,* scientists estimate that 8.8 million tons of plastic enter the ocean every year, threatening over 700 species of marine animals.

Even remote areas such as the Arctic Circle are impacted by man-made pollution. There isn't a single location on Earth that's untouched by plastic pollution.

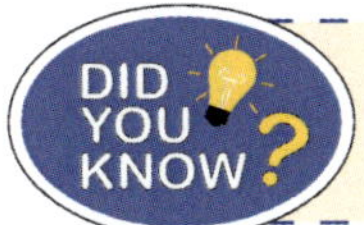

Iceland is growing 5 centimeters per year as the tectonic plates move wider apart. Russia's Trans-Siberian Railway crosses 3,901 bridges.

The Great Pacific Garbage Patch is a huge collection of garbage and debris in the middle of the northern Pacific Ocean, much like a floating island. This "island" of plastic litter and garbage is caught in the water currents. It formed because currents near the center of the northern Pacific Ocean move around in a kind of circle, which catches and holds floating pieces of plastic. The Great Pacific Garbage Patch contains a staggering number of pieces of plastic, estimated to be between 1.1 to 3.6 **trillion**. That's roughly 200 pieces of plastic for every person on the planet!

These tiny particles of plastic, abandoned in the ocean, are terrible news for marine life because they can easily be mistaken for food, and end up being ingested by fish, sea turtles, and mammals. Plastic bags can be particularly tempting to sea turtles, as they closely

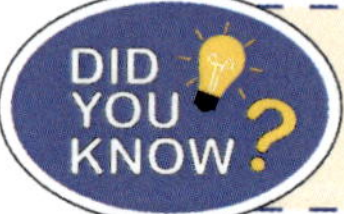

Lesotho, San Marino and Vatican City are the only three countries that are completely landlocked by another country.

resemble a key part of the turtle's diet: jellyfish. As well as ingesting it, sea turtles are also in danger of becoming entangled in plastic. Having their flippers wrapped in plastic can often result in death, as they lose the ability to swim and feed themselves.

Like a soup of plastic pieces floating in the ocean just below the surface, this island is located between Hawaii and Japan. Scientists estimate that the size of this "plastic island" is approximately three times the size of France.

FRIGHTENING FACTS ABOUT POLLUTION

- 40% of the rivers and 46% of the lakes located in the United States are much too polluted for fishing or swimming.
- Approximately 50% of the globe's population has to deal with polluted drinking water.
- Around 250 million toxic occurrences caused by polluted drinking water are reported every year, which leads to anywhere from 5 to 10 million deaths annually.
- According to a recent study, 46% of the Great Pacific Garbage Patch is made up of fishing nets.
- About 70% of the industrial waste generated in developing countries is dumped into the water untreated. This pollutes the potable water in many locations.
- The rise of the carbon footprint and increased greenhouse gases caused by industrial pollution is responsible for global warming. Global warming changes our weather patterns, which can lead to disasters such as cyclones, earthquakes, and the premature melting of the world's glaciers.

PART THREE:
FLEX YOUR GEO-MUSCLES
AND BUILD YOUR GEO-SKILLS

I CAN FIND THESE COUNTRIES ON THE MAP!

Check each country you can find on the map.
Prove it by telling what countries are its neighbors.

Country	Its closest neighbors are:
China	______________________________
India	______________________________
United States	______________________________
Indonesia	______________________________
Pakistan	______________________________
Brazil	______________________________
Nigeria	______________________________
Bangladesh	______________________________
Russia	______________________________

Country	Its closest neighbors are:
Mexico	______________________
Japan	______________________
Ethiopia	______________________
Philippines	______________________
Egypt	______________________
Vietnam	______________________
Demcratic Republic of Congo	______________________
Turkey	______________________
Iran	______________________
Germany	______________________
Thailand	______________________
United Kingdom	______________________
France	______________________
Italy	______________________

Country	Its closest neighbors are:
Tanzania	______________________________
South Africa	______________________________
Myanmar	______________________________
Kenya	______________________________
South Korea	______________________________
Colombia	______________________________
Spain	______________________________
Uganda	______________________________
Argentina	______________________________
Algeria	______________________________
Sudan	______________________________
Ukraine	______________________________
Iraq	______________________________
Afghanistan	______________________________

Country	Its closest neighbors are:
Poland	______________________
Canada	______________________
Morocco	______________________
Saudi Arabia	______________________
Uzbekistan	______________________
Peru	______________________
Angola	______________________
Malaysia	______________________
Mozambique	______________________
Ghana	______________________
Yemen	______________________
Nepal	______________________
Venezuela	______________________
Madagascar	______________________

Country	Its closest neighbors are:
Cameroon	______________________________
Côte d'Ivoire	______________________________
North Korea	______________________________
Australia	______________________________
Niger	______________________________
Sri Lanka	______________________________
Burkina Faso	______________________________
Mali	______________________________
Romania	______________________________
Malawi	______________________________
Chile	______________________________
Kazakhstan	______________________________
Zambia	______________________________
Guatemala	______________________________

Country	Its closest neighbors are:
Ecuador	______________________________
Syria	______________________________
Netherlands	______________________________
Senegal	______________________________
Cambodia	______________________________
Chad	______________________________
Somalia	______________________________
Zimbabwe	______________________________
Guinea	______________________________
Rwanda	______________________________
Benin	______________________________
Burundi	______________________________
Tunisia	______________________________
Bolivia	______________________________

Country	Its closest neighbors are:
Belgium	____________________
Haiti	____________________
Cuba	____________________
South Sudan	____________________
Dominican Republic	____________________
Czech Republic (Czechia)	____________________
Greece	____________________
Jordan	____________________
Portugal	____________________
Azerbaijan	____________________
Sweden	____________________
Honduras	____________________
United Arab Emirates	____________________
Hungary	____________________

Country	Its closest neighbors are:
Tajikistan	------------------------------
Belarus	------------------------------
Austria	------------------------------
Papua New Guinea	------------------------------
Serbia	------------------------------
Israel	------------------------------
Switzerland	------------------------------
Togo	------------------------------
Sierra Leone	------------------------------
Laos	------------------------------
Paraguay	------------------------------
Bulgaria	------------------------------
Libya	------------------------------
Lebanon	------------------------------

Country	Its closest neighbors are:
Nicaragua	------------------------------
Kyrgyzstan	------------------------------
El Salvador	------------------------------
Turkmenistan	------------------------------
Singapore	------------------------------
Denmark	------------------------------
Finland	------------------------------
Congo	------------------------------
Slovakia	------------------------------
Norway	------------------------------
Oman	------------------------------
State of Palestine	------------------------------
Costa Rica	------------------------------
Liberia	------------------------------

Country	Its closest neighbors are:
Ireland	________________________________
Central African Republic	________________________________
New Zealand	________________________________
Mauritania	________________________________
Panama	________________________________
Kuwait	________________________________
Croatia	________________________________
Moldova	________________________________
Georgia	________________________________
Eritrea	________________________________
Uruguay	________________________________
Bosnia and Herzegovina	________________________________
Mongolia	________________________________
Armenia	________________________________

Country	Its closest neighbors are:
Jamaica	______________________________
Qatar	______________________________
Albania	______________________________
Lithuania	______________________________
Namibia	______________________________
Gambia	______________________________
Botswana	______________________________
Gabon	______________________________
Lesotho	______________________________
North Macedonia	______________________________
Slovenia	______________________________
Guinea-Bissau	______________________________
Latvia	______________________________
Bahrain	______________________________

Country	Its closest neighbors are:
Equatorial Guinea	________________________________
Trinidad and Tobago	________________________________
Estonia	________________________________
Timor-Leste	________________________________
Mauritius	________________________________
Cyprus	________________________________
Eswatini (formerly Swaziland)	________________________________
Djibouti	________________________________
Fiji	________________________________
Comoros	________________________________
Guyana	________________________________
Bhutan	________________________________
Solomon Islands	________________________________
Montenegro	________________________________

Country	Its closest neighbors are:
Luxembourg	______________________________
Suriname	______________________________
Cabo Verde	______________________________
Maldives	______________________________
Malta	______________________________
Brunei	______________________________
Belize	______________________________
Bahamas	______________________________
Iceland	______________________________
Vanuatu	______________________________
Barbados	______________________________
Sao Tome & Principe	______________________________
Samoa	______________________________
Saint Lucia	______________________________

Country	Its closest neighbors are:
Kiribati	______________________________
Micronesia	______________________________
Grenada	______________________________
St. Vincent & Grenadines	______________________________
Tonga	______________________________
Seychelles	______________________________
Antigua and Barbuda	______________________________
Andorra	______________________________
Dominica	______________________________
Marshall Islands	______________________________
Saint Kitts & Nevis	______________________________
Monaco	______________________________
Liechtenstein	______________________________
San Marino	______________________________

Country	Its closest neighbors are:
Palau	______________________________
Tuvalu	______________________________
Nauru	______________________________
Holy See (Vatican City)	______________________________

IN WHICH COUNTRY WOULD YOU FIND EACH OF THESE CITIES?

If any of these cities are in the United States, in which state would find that city?

City	In which country or U.S. State) ?
Abidjan	________________
Algiers	________________
Amsterdam	________________
Amman	________________
Ankara	________________
Athens	________________
Atlanta	________________
Auckland	________________
Baghdad	________________

City	In which country or U.S. State) ?
Bangkok	______________________________
Barcelona	______________________________
Beijing	______________________________
Beirut	______________________________
Belgrade	______________________________
Berlin	______________________________
Bern	______________________________
Bogota	______________________________
Bonn	______________________________
Boston	______________________________
Bratislava	______________________________
Brussels	______________________________
Bucharest	______________________________
Budapest	______________________________
Buenos Aires	______________________________

City	In which country or U.S. State) ?
Cairo	______________________________
Calcutta (Kolkata)	______________________________
Calgary	______________________________
Cape Town	______________________________
Caracas	______________________________
Casablanca	______________________________
Chicago	______________________________
Copenhagen	______________________________
Dallas	______________________________
Damascus	______________________________
Detroit	______________________________
Dublin	______________________________
Durban	______________________________
Edinburgh	______________________________
Florence	______________________________

City	In which country or U.S. State)?
Frankfurt	______________________________
Hamburg	______________________________
Harare	______________________________
Havana	______________________________
Helsinki	______________________________
Ho Chi Minh City	______________________________
Honolulu	______________________________
Islamabad	______________________________
Istanbul	______________________________
Jerusalem	______________________________
Jeddah (Jiddah)	______________________________
Johannesburg	______________________________
Kabul	______________________________
Kampala	______________________________
Karachi	______________________________

City	In which country or U.S. State) ?
Kiev (Kiyiv)	
Lago	
La Paz	
Liverpool	
Lisbon	
Ljubljana	
London	
Los Angeles	
Madrid	
Managua	
Manila	
Maputo	
Melbourne	
Mexico City	
Montevideo	

City	In which country or U.S. State) ?
Montreal	_______________
Moscow	_______________
Mumbai (Bombay)	_______________
Nairobi	_______________
Naples	_______________
New Delhi	_______________
New Orleans	_______________
New York City	_______________
Osaka	_______________
Oslo	_______________
Ottawa	_______________
Panama City	_______________
Paris	_______________
Perth	_______________
Philadelphia	_______________

City	In which country or U.S. State) ?
Port au Prince	
Prague	
Pyongyang	
Reykjavik	
Rio de Janeiro	
Riyadh	
St. Louis	
St. Petersburg (not in U.S.)	
San Francisco	
San Jose (U.S.)	
San Jose (another country)	
San Juan	
San Salvador	
Santiago	
Sao Paulo	

City	In which country or U.S. State) ?
Sarajevo	____________________________
Seoul	____________________________
Shanghai	____________________________
Sofia	____________________________
Stockholm	____________________________
Sydney	____________________________
Taipei	____________________________
Tehran	____________________________
Tel Aviv	____________________________
Tirana	____________________________
Tripoli	____________________________
Tokyo	____________________________
Toronto	____________________________
Ulaanbaatar	____________________________
Vancouver	____________________________

City	In which country or U.S. State) ?
Venice	______________________________
Vienna	______________________________
Warsaw	______________________________
Wellington	______________________________
Winnipeg	______________________________
Zagreb	______________________________

WHERE IN EUROPE ARE GRANDMA AND GRANDPA?

Grandma and Grandpa love traveling more than just about anything else. When traveling, you learn so much and you meet many different people from different cultures. You hear lots of languages and you see so many new things. See if you can follow them as they travel from country to country." Here we go!

HINT	CITY AND COUNTRY
1. The grandparents started their trip by flying out of John F. Kennedy International Airport in the largest city in the U.S.	__________________ __________________
2. Soon, they arrived at Heathrow Airport. They drove their rented car on the left side of the road. They saw Big Ben, Westminster Abbey, and Buckingham Palace. That night, they saw a wonderful show in the West End Theater District. Afterward, they strolled down Piccadilly Circus and enjoyed a spot of tea.	__________________ __________________
3. All too soon, they took off again. They landed at Gardermoen International Airport, then left that city and took a boat up a lovely *fjord*, where they saw spectacular glacier mountains.	__________________ __________________
4. Now, it's time for them to head south — but not too far south. From 1948 until 1991, this country was actually *two* countries until it was reunited. A large, ugly wall in this city kept some of its citizens from escaping to the West. Before World War II, it was one of the largest and most splendid cities in Europe. After the war, it was a charred ruin.	__________________ __________________

HINT	CITY AND COUNTRY
6. Heading east, Grandma and Grandpa now approach a city that is so lovely that a famous philosopher once called it "a symphony in stone." It is the capital of the Czech Republic, also called Czechia. It is located on the River Vltava, sometimes known as the Moldau, and it has a huge and wondrous castle known as Hradcany.	___________________ ___________________
7. 150 years ago, the *waltz* was the most popular dance in Europe. A "rock star" of his day, Johann Strauss, Jr., made this city the music capital of the world. Well, he wasn't the only one. Many other famous composers lived in this city on the Danube River: Mozart, Beethoven, Schubert, and Brahms, just to name a few. The *Schönbrunn Palace* and the Spanish Riding School, and the *Musikverein* are great places to visit.	___________________ ___________________
8. Now, the grandparents sail down the Danube River for several hours until they come to the capital of a country where you can eat delicious *gulyas* (goulash) and hear Gypsy violinists play music called *Czardas*. In this country, your first name is actually your *last* name. Thus, this nation's most famous composer would be called "Liszt Franz" instead of Franz Liszt. And this capital city was called *Aquincum* in the days of the ancient Roman Empire.	___________________ ___________________
9. Wow! Grandma and Grandpa land at Atatürk International Airport at the southernmost tip of Europe — in a city that actually sits on *two* continents, Europe and Asia. It's a noisy, exciting place where you'll find 4,000 shops in the Grand Covered Bazaar, Aya Sofia Museum (one of the oldest buildings in the world), the Blue Mosque, the Bosphorus, and the Golden Horn.	___________________ ___________________
10. Time to head west again. Grandma and Grandpa arrive at one of the world's oldest cities. This morning, they climbed the Acropolis and saw the Parthenon. This afternoon, they went to Syntagma Square. This evening, they're going to the *Plaka* and to *Monastiraki*, where they'll eat *souvlaki* and listen to Éntekhno music by the famous composer Manos Hatzidakis.	___________________ ___________________

HINT	CITY AND COUNTRY
11. It's time for Grandma and Grandpa to visit one of their favorite places in Europe, a World Heritage site on the Adriatic Sea. It's a medieval city entirely surrounded by a high wall and they love to walk on top of the wall, and eat delicious seafood in the town itself. This place was once part of a country called Yugoslavia, which no longer exists.	__________________ __________________
12. Grandma and Grandpa cross the Adriatic Sea to the port of Venice. They drive through the Apennine Mountains until they cross the Tiber River and come to one of the most famous cities in the world. In fact, it gave its name to an empire that *owned* an awful lot of the world 2,000 years ago. It's still home to the Colosseum (the Forum), and it marks the beginning of one of the most famous highways in the world, the Appian Way.	__________________ __________________
13. More than 2,000 years ago, a general named Hannibal crossed the Alps with 40 elephants. Today, Grandma and Grandpa are crossing the Alps via the Brenner Pass in a Fiat automobile. They turn west into a country where they see many famous Alpine mountains — the Jungfrau, the Eiger, and the Matterhorn. Finally, they arrive at this country's largest city. When they've traveled from the Alps to this city, they've truly traveled from "A" to "Z."	__________________ __________________
14. Grandma and Grandpa love this country so much that they want to see it once more before they leave Europe. They head east and drive the highest Alpine road in Europe — the Grossglockner, where they stop to walk on a real glacier! Winding down from the summit, they come to this country's second largest city. Mozart was born here and there's a medieval fortress on top of a large mountain right in the center of this city on the Salzach River. The grandparents think it's one of the two most beautiful cities they've ever seen.	__________________ __________________
15. A bit farther north, Grandma and Grandpa come to a big city that is famous for beer halls and Oompa bands. Its name means "the monks," and in the native language it's spelled "M-ü-n-c-h-e-n."	__________________ __________________

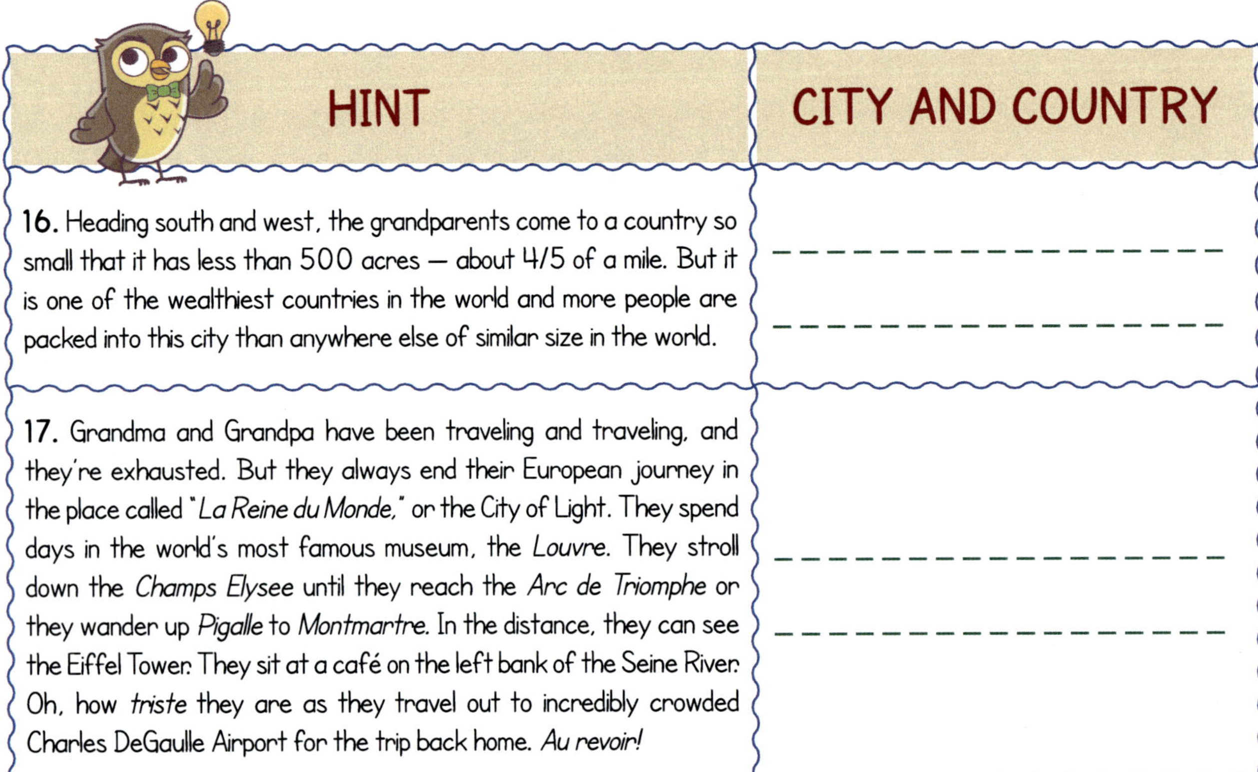

HINT	CITY AND COUNTRY
16. Heading south and west, the grandparents come to a country so small that it has less than 500 acres — about 4/5 of a mile. But it is one of the wealthiest countries in the world and more people are packed into this city than anywhere else of similar size in the world.	________________ ________________
17. Grandma and Grandpa have been traveling and traveling, and they're exhausted. But they always end their European journey in the place called "*La Reine du Monde,*" or the City of Light. They spend days in the world's most famous museum, the *Louvre*. They stroll down the *Champs Elysee* until they reach the *Arc de Triomphe* or they wander up *Pigalle* to *Montmartre*. In the distance, they can see the Eiffel Tower. They sit at a café on the left bank of the Seine River. Oh, how *triste* they are as they travel out to incredibly crowded Charles DeGaulle Airport for the trip back home. *Au revoir!*	________________ ________________

ANSWERS TO WHERE IN EUROPE ARE GRANDMA AND GRANDPA

1. New York City, U.S.A.
2. London, England (United Kingdom)
3. Oslo, Norway
4. Berlin, Germany
5. Dublin, Ireland
6. Prague, Czech Republic (Czechia)
7. Vienna, Austria
8. Budapest, Hungary
9. Istanbul, Turkey
10. Athens, Greece
11. Dubrovnik, Croatia
12. Rome, Italy
13. Zurich, Switzerland
14. Salzburg, Austria
15. Munich, Germany
16. Monte Carlo, Monaco
17. Paris, France

WHERE IN THE UNITED STATES ARE GRANDMA AND GRANDPA?

Grandma and Grandpa love traveling in their own country as much as anyplace else. There are lots of fabulous, interesting places here. Where are they visiting in each place listed below?

HINT	CITY AND STATE
1. You won't find Disneyland here, but you will find Disney World, Epcot Center, and Lake Buena Vista. The Cape Kennedy Space Center in nearby Cape Canaveral is less than an hour away in this very flat, finger shaped state.	________________ ________________
2. Get your "Rocky Mountain High" here as you watch the Broncos play football and the Rockies play baseball. The Rocky Mountains are to the west and the Great Plains start to the east of this "Mile High City."	________________ ________________
3. This East Coast city was one of the largest in the U.S. in the early days. The Pilgrims landed at Plymouth Rock. Harvard University is in adjacent Cambridge. The Red Sox play baseball here, and the New England Patriots play from this area.	________________ ________________
4. If you can make it here, you'll make it anywhere! This is *it* — The Big Apple, Broadway and Manhattan, Brooklyn and Queens, Harlem, the Bowery, Wall Street, and the Statue of Liberty. Let's face it, this is simply the #1 city in the U.S.A.	________________ ________________
5. No big cities in the center of the country? Think again. This is the 4th most populous city in the U.S.A. Home of the Texans football team, the Astros baseball team, and a handful of Bushes.	________________ ________________

HINT	CITY AND STATE
6. This northwest city, named after a Native American leader who preached ecology and saving the Earth for all, has the Space Needle and the Pike Street Market. Nearby are the headquarters of such industry giants as Boeing, Microsoft, Costco, Amazon, and Starbucks.	___________________ ___________________
7. Grandma and Grandpa just flew into Sky Harbor Airport in the Valley of the Sun. They've driven through Tempe and Scottsdale on their way into the fifth largest city in the U.S., home of one of the most extensive music museums in the world, Camelback Mountain, and nearby Luke Air Force Base.	___________________ ___________________
8. The "Gateway Arch," located on the West Bank of the Mississippi River, commemorates the pioneer days when this city was known as the "Gateway to the West."	___________________ ___________________
9. This is also a "gateway city," but for different groups of people. It's the only major U.S. city founded by a woman. Although this city is in the United States, it is known as the "Capital of the Caribbean."	___________________ ___________________
10. This town is not "New" at all. To many visitors, "The Big Easy" is their favorite entertainment venue in the U.S., what with Mardi Gras, Bourbon Street, the French Quarter, and many of the original streetcars from the 1920s still running. "*Laissez les bon temps rouler!*"	___________________ ___________________
11. For a long time it was called the "Second City." Now it is now the third largest city by population in the U.S. Called the "Windy City," both because of the fierce winds that blow off Lake Michigan and because of the notorious bluster of its politicians. Home of the Cubs, the White Sox, the Bulls, and the Bears, as well as myriad museums and O'Hare Airport.	___________________ ___________________

HINT	CITY AND STATE
12. More than a hundred years ago, this tiny town had a very big name, *"Nuestra Señora La Reina de Los Angeles de Porciuncula."* But then they started making movies here and this city grew and grew until it became "The Big Orange," the second largest city in America. With Hollywood, Disneyland, and a glorious year-round climate, who could ask for more?	________________ ________________
13. Just before the Revolutionary War, this was the largest city in the U.S., home to Ben Franklin and the Liberty Bell. Today it boasts the Eagles, the Phillies, and South Street.	________________ ________________
14. The "Twin Cities" get very cold in winter and very warm in summer. The "Mall of America" is so huge there's a full-blown amusement park complete with a roller coaster *inside* the mall.	________________ ________________
15. This city on the Potomac River, surrounded by two states, Maryland and Virginia, is (at least temporarily) home to lots of famous people, the most famous of whom lives in the White House.	________________ ________________
16. The largest city in the southeastern United States, Martin Luther King, Jr., preached here. Early during the Civil Rights movement, it called itself "the city that's too busy to hate." It's home to Hartsfield-Jackson International Airport, the world's largest airline hub.	________________ ________________
17. One of the fastest growing cities in the United States, "Music City U.S.A.," is home to the Grand Ole Opry, a large segment of America's Medical business, and the home of the 7th U.S. president, Andrew Jackson.	________________ ________________
18. This Midwestern city is located in *two* states. It's a city of rolling hills, famous barbecue, and blues music. The cities of each state are separately incorporated but are part of the same metropolitan area. Walt Disney started his first animation studio, which went bankrupt, in this city before he moved to California.	________________ ________________

HINT	CITY AND STATE
19. The American automobile industry began here, and this city is still called "Motown." In the early days, it was a major arts and culture center, but it has fallen on hard days in the past 50 years and is still trying valiantly to restore its former glory times.	___________________ ___________________
20. If you live in Northern California, there's only one place that's truly called "The City." It's also been called Baghdad by the Bay, the City on Seven Hills, and the Barbary Coast. Little cable cars climb halfway to the stars, and be sure you visit North Beach, Chinatown, Golden Gate Park, Fisherman's Wharf, and Union Square. It's reputed to be everyone's "second favorite city in the U.S."	___________________ ___________________

ANSWERS TO WHERE IN THE UNITED STATES ARE GRANDMA AND GRANDPA

1. Orlando, Florida
2. Denver, Colorado
3. Boston, Massachusetts
4. New York, New York
5. Houston, Texas
6. Seattle, Washington
7. Phoenix, Arizona
8. St. Louis, Missouri
9. Miami, Florida
10. New Orleans, Louisiana
11. Chicago, Illinois
12. Los Angeles, California
13. Philadelphia, Pennsylvania
14. Minneapolis - St. Paul, Minnesota
15. Washington, D.C.
16. Atlanta, Georgia
17. Nashville, Tennessee
18. Kansas City, Kansas & Kansas City, Missouri
19. Detroit, Michigan
20. San Francisco, California

WHERE IN THE WORLD ARE GRANDMA AND GRANDPA?

Grandma and Grandpa have traveled in the U.S.A. and they've traveled through Europe. Now they want to see parts of the rest of the world because they want to learn even more than they already know. They'll stay in touch with you through WhatsApp and Skype, and they'll send you digital pictures each night so you can keep up with them on their journey.

HINT	CITY AND COUNTRY
1. This city is home to three major world religions. Some of the famous places in this country are the Jordan River, the Sea of Galilee, the Dome of the Rock, and the Negev Desert.	________________ ________________
2. G'day mate! The Opera House in this city looks like a rocket ship — sort of. The country is almost as big as the U.S.A. but has less than 1/10 as many people. In fact, some folks say there are more sheep than people here.	________________ ________________
3. Many years ago, people pronounced the capital of this country 'pē-'kiŋ (Peking). Today, it has more people than any other country in the world and the Great Wall — the only man-made object on Earth that you can see from space — passes near here. The "Forbidden City" is part of is metropolitan area.	________________ ________________
4. This country used to be called "Siam," and its beaches in the south and its amazingly diverse food are magnets for millions of tourists. But this busy, crowded, smoky capital city is one of the most densely packed in the world.	________________ ________________

HINT	CITY AND COUNTRY
5. This country actually has three capitals, but its largest city is not one of them. It's the most populous country in the southern part of Africa, and its Kruger Park, which is larger than the country of Wales, has more animals than people. The large city Grandma and Grandpa are visiting is built on hills that have more gold than almost any other country in the world.	________________ ________________
6. They build the Toyota and many other kinds of motors near this capital city, the most populous in the world with more than 38 million people. It used to be called "Edo," it has a huge business area known as the Ginza.	________________ ________________
7. This great ancient city on the River Nile is close to the Pyramids of Giza and the Sphinx. It is very hot and dry.	________________ ________________
8. The Tigris and Euphrates, two great rivers of antiquity, start in this country. The country is 97% in Asia and 3% in Europe. It is said that this country has more historical structures than the rest of Europe put together, but its present capital city was only a dusty village in the 1920s. Today, this city has more than 5 million people.	________________ ________________
9. This city is at the very top of the North Island of the country, which is made up of two main islands. People who live here are nicknamed "Kiwis," although the native people are called Maoris. This small country is one of the most dramatically beautiful countries in the world.	________________ ________________
10. There are two major deserts in this dry and mountainous country, as well as a famous mountain pass called the Khyber Pass. It has been a country where wars have been fought for more than a thousand years, and its capital city begins with "K."	________________ ________________
11. This country was known throughout history as Persia, but it has a different name today. It is an Islamic Republic and its most powerful leader is the Ayatollah. Grandma and Grandpa saw the Elburz mountain range from its capital and largest city.	________________ ________________

HINT	CITY AND COUNTRY
12. The country to the north of this one has a very closed society, and its capital is Pyongyang. This city of 10 million people is the capital of a country famous for building Hyundai and Kia motor vehicles and LG appliances.	________________ ________________
13. This small island country lies south of India. It is famous for tea and it used to be called "Ceylon." Its capital, which has one of the longest names of any capital in the world, Sri Jayawardenepura Kotte, is a satellite of this larger city.	________________ ________________
14. Nearly 77,000 people per square mile live in this most densely populated city on Earth. It used to have a different name. By the way, the *second* most densely populated city in the whole world, with 62,000 people per square mile, is in the same country.	________________ ________________
15. The border of two countries runs across the summit of Mount Everest, the highest point above sea level on Earth. Which two countries share the summit of Mount Everest?	________________ ________________
16. The lowest land area on Earth is the shoreline of the Dead Sea. Which three countries share the shores of the Dead Sea?	________________ ________________

ANSWERS TO WHERE IN WORLD ARE GRANDMA AND GRANDPA

1. Jerusalem, Israel
2. Sydney, Australia
3. Beijing, China
4. Bangkok, Thailand
5. Johannesburg, South Africa
6. Tokyo, Japan
7. Cairo, Egypt
8. Ankara, Turkey
9. Auckland, New Zealand
10. Kabul, Afghanistan
11. Tehran, Iran
12. Seoul, South Korea
13. Colombo, Sri Lanka
14. Mumbai, India
15. Nepal and China (Tibet)
16. Israel, Jordan, and Syria

TEST YOUR GEO-Q #1

1. Ferdinand Magellan was the first European to sail across the ocean he called by a name that means "Peaceful." What is the name of this ocean?

____

2. The point where the boundaries of Arizona, Colorado, New Mexico, and Utah meet is popularly known by what name?

____

3. Farming in Egypt is concentrated along what river?

____

4. Most of the world's highest mountains (from the Earth's land surface) are part of this mountain system.

____

5. To fly from Madrid, Spain, to Rome, Italy, in what cardinal direction would you travel?

____

6. Ships use the Suez Canal to avoid sailing around which continent?

____

7. Name the largest country in the West Indies (Caribbean).

____

8. How many continents are there? ____ Name them: __________________

____

____

9. Name four (4) oceans:

10. Name three (3) seas:

11. In which hemisphere is the Tropic of Cancer?

12. In which hemisphere is the Tropic of Capricorn?

13. What is the highest mountain peak on Earth measured from the Earth's land surface?

14. What is a peninsula?

15. What is the highest peak in North America *and* in which state is it found?

16. Name the seven (7) countries that make up Central America:

17. What is the name of a famous canal built through a country in Central America?

____

18. Name two agricultural products grown in Central America:

____________________ and ____________________

19. What European "discovered" the West Indies?

____

20. Name the only countries in South America that do not touch Brazil.

____

ANSWERS TO TEST YOUR GEO-Q #1

1. Pacific
2. The four corners area
3. The Nile
4. The Himalayas
5. East
6. Africa
7. Cuba
8. North America, South America, Europe, Asia, Africa, Australia, Antarctica
9. Atlantic, Pacific, Indian, Arctic
10. Mediterranean, Caribbean, Adriatic, Aegean, Black, Caspian, Red, Baltic, Marmara
11. Northern
12. Southern
13. Mount Everest
14. A piece of land surrounded on three sides by water
15. Mount Denali (also called Mount McKinley), Alaska
16. Guatemala, Belize, Honduras, El Salvador, Nicaragua, Costa Rica, Panama
17. The Panama Canal
18. Coffee, bananas, sugar
19. Christopher Columbus
20. Chile and Ecuador Chile

TEST YOUR GEO-Q #2

1. What is the largest country in the world that borders only one other country?

____

2. Which continent is almost cut in half by the equator?

____

3. Which island is the world's fourth largest and off the coast of Africa?

____

4. What desert in Africa covers an area larger than the continental U.S.?

____

5. What is the highest mountain in Africa, and in which country is it?

____

6. What two countries are partly in Europe and partly in Africa?

____

7. What is the name of the mountain range between Spain and France?

____

8. On what river is Paris, France situated?

____

9. Name three (3) capitals situated on the Danube River:

____

10. Name the sea between Italy and Croatia:

____

11. Name the sea between Greece and Turkey:

____

12. Name the tiny country in the Pyrenees Mountains between Spain and France:

____

13. Lake Geneva is on the border of which two European countries?

____________________ and ____________________

14. What continent has 60% of the world's population?

____

15. One of the world's great deserts is found in Mongolia. Name it:

____

16. A region in Southwestern Asia rich in petroleum deposits lies between two rivers that were mentioned in the Bible. Name the two rivers:

____________________ and ____________________

17. Name two rivers in China that begin with the letter "Y":

________________________ and ________________________

18. The largest mountain in the world from base to summit is not the highest mountain on the Earth's surface because it is measured from the bottom of the ocean. What is its name and where would you find it?

____

19. The longest continuous river system in the United States consists of two rivers that connect to one another. Name them:

________________________ and ________________________

20. Name the five Great Lakes of the United States:

____

ANSWERS TO TEST YOUR GEO-Q #2

1. Canada
2. Africa
3. Madagascar
4. Sahara Desert
5. Kilimanjaro, Tanzania
6. Russia, Turkey
7. The Pyrenees
8. The Seine
9. Vienna, Bratislava, Budapest, Belgrade
10. Adriatic
11. Aegean
12. Andorra
13. Switzerland and France
14. Asia
15. Gobi Desert
16. Tigris and Euphrates
17. Yellow and Yangtze
18. Mauna Kea, Hawaii
19. Mississippi - Missouri
20. Superior, Michigan, Erie, Huron, Ontario

TEST YOUR GEO-Q #3

1. Name three large cities in India:

____

2. Atlanta is the largest city in the U.S. state of _______________________

3. _______________________ is the largest state by area in the United States.

4. The longest river in Europe is the _______________________________

5. Name four (4) rivers in Africa:

____

____

6. The name of the largest mountain range in South America is:

____

7. There are some islands in the world that are inhabited by two countries. Name any two countries that share the same island:

____

8. What countries border the Sea of Marmara?

____

9. Lyonnaise potatoes is a famous dish in this country. Even though it's spelled "N-i-c-e," a large city in this country is pronounced "Niece." People who live in its largest city are called Parisians. Name the country:

_________________________ and _________________________

10. Mrs. Gerstl went to the Opera at La Scala. She loved it! Leonardo's famous painting *The Last Supper* can be found in this city. Name the city and the country:

____

11. *The Beautiful Blue Danube, Tales from the Vienna Woods, The Emperors' Waltz,* and *Die Fledermaus* were all written by a composer named Johann Strauss, Jr. In what city and country did he live and work?

____

12. Ho Chi Minh is a national hero in this country. The main road in this country was called "The Ho Chi Minh Trail," and its largest city used to be called Saigon. Name the country: _____________________ Name two cities in this country:

_________________________ and _________________________

13. Which are the only two countries in South America that do not touch an ocean?

_________________________ and _________________________

14. This is the longest, skinniest country in South America – probably in the world. It's named ____

15. Abu Dhabi is one of the United Arab Emirates. Name two others:

_________________________ and _________________________

16. Which of the United States is the farthest west? (Hint: Use latitude and longitude to help you.)

____

17. Which of the United States is the farthest east?

____

18. Which of the United States is the farthest north?

____

____

19. Which of the United States is the farthest south?

____

20. The Mississippi River and the Ohio River join at a town in the U.S. that has the same spelling as a famous ancient city in Egypt. Name the city and the state:

____

ANSWERS TO TEST YOUR GEO-Q #3

1. New Delhi, Mumbai, Kolkata, Chennai, Bangalore, Hyderabad, Ahmedabad, Pune
2. Georgia
3. Alaska
4. Danube
5. Nile, Congo, Zambezi, Orange, Niger, Vaal, Limpopo, Ubangi, Tugela
6. The Andes
7. Hispaniola: Haiti and Dominican Republic; New Guinea: Indonesia and Brunei; Borneo: Malaysia, Indonesia, and Brunei; Cyprus: Cyprus (Greece) and Turkish Republic of Northern Cyprus
8. Turkey. It's the only one.
9. France
10. Milan, Italy
11. Vienna, Austria
12. Ho Chi Minh City (formerly Saigon); Hanoi; Haiphong; Hue; Da Nang.
13. Bolivia and Paraguay
14. Chile
15. Ajman, Dubai, Fujairah, Ras Al Khaimah, Sharjah and Umm Al Quwain.
16. West: Alaska
17. East: Maine
18. North: Alaska
19. South: Hawaii
20. Cairo, Illinois

TEST YOUR GEO-Q #4

1. A land of dikes, windmills, tulips, and Rembrandt. One name for this country is Holland. Its other name is ______________________________

2. The United Kingdom actually contains four countries on two islands. What are the names of these countries?

______________________, ______________________,

______________________, and ______________________

3. Name any four (4) large cities in the world that are on or very near to latitude 40° north:

____

____

4. What is the largest country by area in South America? ______________

What is the smallest? ______________________________

5. Since this island nation is heated by hundreds of hot springs, it is comfortable, even though you'd think by its name it's very cold.

____

6. This city sits directly on the equator! Name the city and the country of which it is the capital.

____

7. These beautiful islands, which used to be called "The Sandwich Islands," became the 50th state on August 21, 1959. Name each of the major inhabited islands in this group.

____

____

8. We have 50 states. Canada, our neighbor to the north, has 12 provinces. Name them:

____

____

____

____

____

9. South Africa is the only country with three capitals – a legislative capital (where the laws are made), an executive capital (where the president lives), and a judicial capital (where they have the Supreme Court). Name all three capitals:

Legislative: ___________________________________

Executive: ___________________________________

Judicial: ___________________________________

10. An Ambassador is a man or woman who represents his or her country in another country. Tell us the names of the countries where each of the ambassadors who lives in these cities would be:

Vienna: ___________________________________

Gaborone: ___________________________________

Judicial: ___________________________________

Nur-Sultan: ___________________________________

11. Four countries and one dependency share the Iberian Peninsula. They are:

---

12. A few years ago, Mr. & Mrs. Gerstl traveled through the entire Balkan Peninsula. Which countries did they visit?

---

13. In 1997, the British Crown Colony on the south coast of China became part of China. What is it called?

---

14. This country used to be called Burma. What is its name today?

---

15. Vientiane is the capital of what southeast Asian country?

---

16. People who come from this country used to be called Moors. Its largest city gave its name to a famous movie made way back in 1942. Name the country and its largest city.

---

17. This large city in a small western European country has a famous statue of a little boy going to the bathroom! It also gave its name to a green vegetable that looks and tastes like a small cabbage. Name the city and the country.

---

18. This is the largest island in the world that is <u>not</u> a continent. What is its name?

---

19. There are lots of huge countries in Africa but there are also lots of tiny ones. Name five (5) of the smallest:

----

20. This country has two "rulers." One lives in France and the other lives in Spain. The people who live in this country are called "Basques," and it is one of the oldest countries in Europe. What is its name?

ANSWERS TO TEST YOUR GEO-Q #4

1. Netherlands
2. England, Scotland, Wales, and Northern Ireland
3. San Francisco, Salt Lake City, Kansas City, Pittsburgh, Cincinnati, Baltimore, Philadelphia, Madrid (Spain), Naples (Italy), Ankara (Turkey), Yerevan (Armenia), Samarkand (Uzbekistan), Baku (Azerbaijan), Beijing (China), Pyongyang (North Korea)'
4. Brazil is the largest. Suriname is the smallest.
5. Iceland
6. Quito, Ecuador
7. Hawaii, Oahu, Maui, Lanai, Molokai, Kauai, Niihau
8. Alberta, British Columbia, Manitoba, New Brunswick, Newfoundland, Nova Scotia, Ontario, Prince Edward Island, Quebec, Saskatchewan, Northwest Territories, Yukon Territory
9. Legislative: Cape Town - Executive: Pretoria - Judicial: Bloemfontein
10. Vienna, Austria; Gaborone, Botswana; Bucharest, Romania; Nur-Sultan, Kazakhstan
11. Spain, Portugal, Andorra, a small part of southern France, and the British dependency of Gibraltar
12. Romania, Moldova, Bulgaria, Serbia, Croatia, Slovenia, Bosnia & Herzegovina, Kosovo, Montenegro, Albania, Macedonia, Greece, and the European part of Turkey
13. Hong Kong
14. Myanmar
15. Laos
16. The country is Morocco. Its largest city is Casablanca.
17. Brussels, Belgium
18. Greenland
19. Countries on the continent: The Gambia, Eswatini (formerly Swaziland), Djibouti, Rwanda, Burundi, Equatorial Guinea, Lesotho, Guinea-Bissau, and Togo. Island countries off the coast of Africa, which are considered part of Africa include: Seychelles, São Tomé and Príncipe, Mauritius, Comoros, Cape Verde
20. Andorra

TEST YOUR GEO-Q #5

1. Which three states lie completely above latitude 45° north?

____

2. If Jessica drives from the capital of North Dakota to the capital of Washington state, how many states will she pass through? _______ Name them:

____

3. Henry left Cheyenne, Wyoming, and traveled 200 miles due east. Then he traveled 200 miles due south. What state was he in when he stopped traveling?

____

4. This state has the smallest population in the U.S., smaller even than Washington D.C.

____

5. The largest of the Great Lakes touches three states. Name the lake and name the states:

____

____

6. Tristyn traveled the entire length of the Rio Grande River. How many states does that river touch? _______ Name them:

____

7. This is the only state that is split by a body of water:

____

8. Tom lives in the largest city in Northern California. His cousin Angela lives in a mid-western state, the capital of which is the last name of a famous U.S. president. If Tom flies directly to his cousin's home, which states will he fly over?

____

____

____

9. Carrie lives in a state that has a foreign country on its border, the most populous state next door, and a famous canyon in the northern part of the state. What is its name?

____

10. Which of the following is <u>not</u> a city in the state of Georgia – Athens, Miami, Atlanta, or Columbus?

____

11. Which of the following states has a desert in it: California, Minnesota, Nevada, Florida, Washington, Pennsylvania, New Mexico, or Arizona?

____

12. Molly lives in a state that has a large river, a great lake, and the "Dairy State" as parts of its border. What is the name of the state where Molly lives and what is the largest city in that state?

____

13. Tara lives in a state that has the same name as the longest river in the United States. What is the name of the capital of Tara's state and the name of the state directly east of Tara's state?

____

14. Two state capitals are located on the Mississippi River. What are their names?

____________________ and ____________________

and what are the two states of which they are the capitals?

____________________ and ____________________

15. Which states border the Gulf of Mexico?

____

____

16. In which direction would you go to travel from Austin, Texas, to Little Rock, Arkansas?

____

17. What direction would you take to go from the capital city of Italy to the largest city in England?

____

18. Which of the following cities is the farthest west: Los Angeles, Reno, San Diego, or Las Vegas?

____

19. The line of latitude numbered 0° is also known as:

____

20. What is the other name for 180° longitude?

____

ANSWERS TO TEST YOUR GEO-Q #5

1. Washington, North Dakota, Alaska
2. Four: North Dakota, Montana, Idaho, Washington
3. Kansas
4. Wyoming
5. Lake Superior touches Minnesota, Wisconsin, and Michigan
6. Three: Colorado, New Mexico, and Texas
7. Michigan
8. California, Nevada, Utah, Colorado, Nebraska (from San Jose, CA to Lincoln, NE)
9. Arizona
10. Miami (Florida)
11. California, New Mexico, Arizona, and New Mexico
12. Illinois
13. Jackson (Mississippi); Alabama
14. St. Paul, Minnesota and Baton Rouge, Louisiana
15. Texas, Louisiana, Mississippi, Alabama, and Florida
16. NE (Northeast)
17. NW (Northwest)
18. Reno
19. The equator
20. The International Date Line

TEST YOUR GEO-Q #6

1. What continent is located in the Northern, Southern, and Western Hemispheres?

____

2. Which of the following is closest to Lima, Peru: the Arctic Circle, the Tropic of Cancer, the equator, or the Tropic of Capricorn?

____

3. Which of the following cities is the farthest <u>east</u>: Miami, Florida; Philadelphia, Pennsylvania; Atlanta, Georgia; or Washington, D.C.?

____

4. Longitude 120° West forms the boundary of which two states?

____________________ and ____________________

5. In what direction would you travel to go from the capital of Canada to the capital of the United States?

____

6. Which countries would you fly over if you traveled directly by plane from Mumbai to Tokyo?

____

7. Stefan sails east through the Strait of Gibraltar. What body of water is he entering?

____

8. Which two bodies of water form part of the border of Egypt?

____

9. What is the only Central American country whose name begins with a vowel?

____

10. What country is bordered by the Coral Sea, the Indian Ocean, and the Pacific Ocean? Its closest neighbor is New Zealand.

____

11. The largest river by volume in the world has its mouth within this country's borders.

____

12. What continent is bordered by the Pacific, Indian, and Arctic Oceans?

____

13. Which of the following South American capitals lies farthest <u>west</u>: Bogota, Sucre, Quito, or Santiago?

____

14. Clarence lives in a country that borders the Atlantic Ocean, the Mediterranean Sea, and the Rhine River as parts of its borders. What country is located due <u>east</u> of the capital of Clarence's country?

____

15. Which two bodies of water does the Panama Canal connect?

____________________ and ____________________

16. Which of the following cities is <u>not</u> located on the west coast of its respective country: Vancouver, Perth, Rome, or Buenos Aires?

____

17. Which of the following words is not used in the name of a state: North, South, East, or West?

____

18. Which of the following states has the Atlantic Ocean as part of its border: Virginia, Vermont, Michigan, or Alabama?

____

19. In a list of the five largest states, which of the following would not belong: Alaska, California, New York, Texas, or Montana?

____

20. Marta lives in a country bordered by the Black Sea, the Danube River, Turkey, Greece, Macedonia, and a country whose capital is Belgrade. What is the name of the capital to the north of Marta's country? ________________________

What is the name of Marta's country? ________________________

ANSWERS TO TEST YOUR GEO-Q #6

1. South America
2. The equator
3. Philadelphia, Pennsylvania
4. California and Nevada
5. South
6. India, Bangladesh, Myanmar (Burma), China, Japan
7. Mediterranean Sea
8. Mediterranean Sea and Red Sea
9. El Salvador
10. Australia
11. Brazil
12. Asia
13. Quito
14. Germany (Clarence's country is France)
15. Pacific Ocean and Caribbean Sea
16. Buenos Aires
17. East
18. Virginia
19. New York
20. The capital to the north of Marta's country is Bucharest (Romania). Marta's country is Bulgaria.

COMMANDER'S ADVANCED QUIZ #1

1. What countries border Spain?

2. What sea lies between Australia and New Zealand?

3. What major U.S. city is served by Dulles International Airport?

4. Ulaanbaatar is the capital of what country?

5. What is the capital of Ecuador?

6. What country has the most time zones? How many?

7. What is the largest lake in Africa?

8. What is the longest river in the Americas?

9. What mountains separate Europe from Asia?

COMMANDER'S ADVANCED QUIZ #1

10. What is the smallest state in surface area in the U.S.? The largest?

---

11. In what city would you find Gorky Park?

---

12. Where would you be if you landed at Dum Dum Airport?

---

13. In what city would you be if you were feeding the pigeons on Piazza San Marco?

---

14. What is the warmest continent?

---

15. What body of water does the Ganges River flow into?

---

16. What is the oldest city in the United States?

---

17. What European city would you be in if you wanted to stroll on the Via Veneto?

COMMANDER'S ADVANCED QUIZ #1

18. What is the only U.S. state that ends with the letter "K?"

____

19. Name four U.S. states that start with the letter "I."

____

20. What body of water does Mauritania border?

____

ANSWERS TO COMMANDER'S ADVANCED QUIZ #1

1. France, Portugal, and Andorra
2. The Tasman Sea
3. Washington, D.C.
4. Mongolia
5. Quito
6. Russia - eleven (11)
7. Lake Victoria
8. The Amazon
9. The Urals
10. Rhode Island; Alaska
11. Moscow
12. Kolkata (Calcutta), India
13. Venice, Italy
14. Africa
15. The Bay of Bengal
16. St. Augustine, Florida
17. Rome, Italy
18. New York
19. Idaho, Illinois, Indiana, Iowa
20. The Atlantic Ocean

COMMANDER'S ADVANCED QUIZ #2

1. What is the smallest country in surface area in Central America?

---

2. What country has more people per square mile than any other country in the world?

---

3. What is the holy city of the Islamic religion?

---

4. Which U.S. state is across Lake Michigan from the city of Milwaukee, Wisconsin?

---

5. What U.S. state includes the San Juan Islands?

---

6. Where in the Americas is it only 47 miles from the Pacific Ocean to the Caribbean Sea?

---

7. What is the only U.S. state whose name ends with three vowels?

---

8. What is the second largest island in the world?

---

9. What is the largest island in Europe?

COMMANDER'S ADVANCED QUIZ #2

10. What city is the farthest north: Milwaukee, Minneapolis, or Toronto?

____

11. What sea surrounds the Cayman Islands?

____

12. What sea lies between Italy and Croatia?

____

13. What two countries are separated by the Gulf of Bothnia?

____

14. What is the second largest continent?

____

15. Where did cable cars first roll down Clay Street in 1873?

____

16. What sea separates Naples and Algiers?

____

17. What body of water forms the world's largest gulf?

____

18. What is the name of India's sacred river?

____

COMMANDER'S ADVANCED QUIZ #2

19. What city's main street is the Grand Canal?

____

20. In what city would you find the Luxembourg Gardens?

____

ANSWERS TO COMMANDER'S ADVANCED QUIZ #2

1. El Salvador
2. Monaco
3. Mecca, Saudi Arabia
4. Michigan
5. Washington
6. Panama
7. Hawaii
8. New Guinea
9. Great Britain
10. Minneapolis
11. The Caribbean Sea
12. The Adriatic Sea
13. Finland and Sweden
14. Africa
15. San Francisco, California
16. The Mediterranean Sea
17. The Gulf of Mexico
18. The Ganges River
19. Venice, Italy
20. Paris, France

CAPTAIN'S ADVANCED QUIZ #1

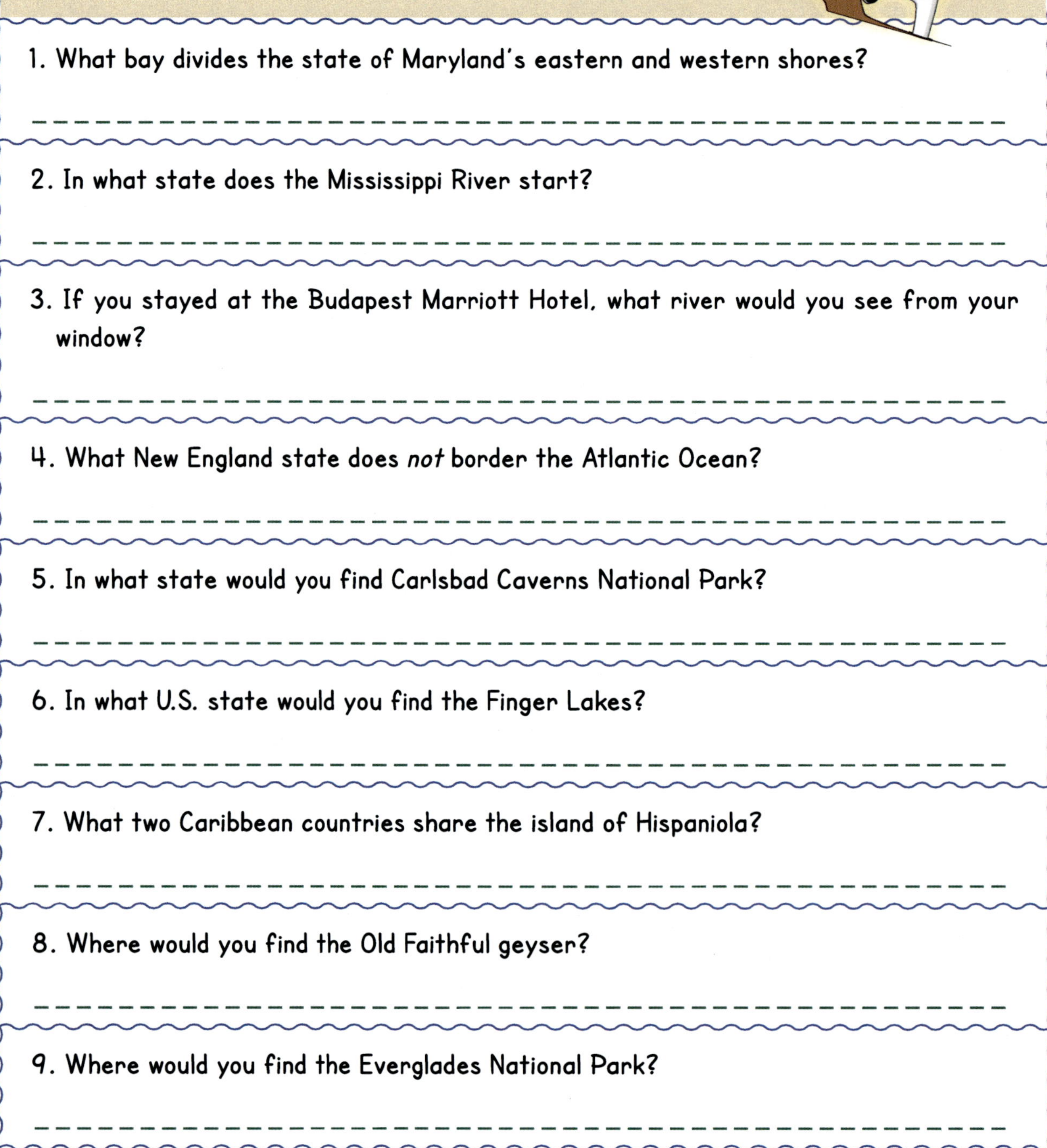

1. What bay divides the state of Maryland's eastern and western shores?

2. In what state does the Mississippi River start?

3. If you stayed at the Budapest Marriott Hotel, what river would you see from your window?

4. What New England state does *not* border the Atlantic Ocean?

5. In what state would you find Carlsbad Caverns National Park?

6. In what U.S. state would you find the Finger Lakes?

7. What two Caribbean countries share the island of Hispaniola?

8. Where would you find the Old Faithful geyser?

9. Where would you find the Everglades National Park?

CAPTAIN'S ADVANCED QUIZ #1

10. What is the largest lake in the Americas?

11. What country consists mainly of the Jutland Peninsula?

12. What country's capital is Tripoli?

13. What is the largest lake in South America?

14. How many U.S. states border the Pacific Ocean? Which ones are they?

15. On what coast of Australia would you find the city of Sydney?

16. What sea would you find between Turkey and Greece?

17. What U.S. state has the longest border with Canada?

CAPTAIN'S ADVANCED QUIZ #1

18. What do Mykonos, Hydra, Samos, and Lesbos have in common?

----

19. In what country would you find Timbuktu?

----

20. What U.S. state capital was named for Kit Carson?

ANSWERS TO CAPTAIN'S ADVANCED QUIZ #1

1. Chesapeake Bay
2. Minnesota
3. The Danube River
4. Vermont
5. New Mexico
6. New York
7. Haiti and the Dominican Republic
8. Yellowstone National Park, Wyoming
9. Florida
10. Lake Superior
11. Denmark
12. Libya
13. Lake Maracaibo
14. Five: California, Oregon, Washington, Alaska, and Hawaii
15. The East Coast
16. The Aegean Sea
17. Alaska
18. They are all Greek islands in the Aegean Sea
19. Mali
20. Carson City, Nevada

CAPTAIN'S ADVANCED QUIZ #2

1. Where is Mount Olympus?

---

2. What independent country is entirely surrounded by the city of Rome?

---

3. Which strait lies between the Atlantic Ocean and the Mediterranean Sea?

---

4. What are the only active volcanoes in Europe?

---

5. What city was the first home to the Statue of Liberty?

---

6. What is the only man-made object on Earth that can be seen from the moon?

---

7. What city's old quarter is called the Plaka?

---

8. Where is Bantry Bay?

---

9. What is the name of the archipelago at the southern tip of South America?

CAPTAIN'S ADVANCED QUIZ #2

10. What ocean surrounds the Sargasso Sea?

____

11. What is the largest country entirely within the Southern Hemisphere?

____

12. What country contains the easternmost point in South America?

____

13. What is the most populous city in South America?

____

14. At a certain ridge in the Rocky Mountains, all the rivers west of that point flow into the Pacific Ocean and all the rivers east of that point flow into the Atlantic Ocean. What is that ridge called?

____

15. What is the highest mountain in the United States?

____

16. On what river would you find the Hoover Dam?

____

17. What river flows at the bottom of the Grand Canyon?

____

CAPTAIN'S ADVANCED QUIZ #2

18. What is the capital of Florida?

____

19. What mountains form the spine of Italy?

____

20. What mountains would you find in Switzerland?

____

ANSWERS TO CAPTAIN'S ADVANCED QUIZ #2

1. Greece
2. The Holy See (also known as Vatican City)
3. The Strait of Gibraltar
4. Mount Vesuvius and Mount Etna
5. Paris, France (It was erected there.)
6. The Great Wall of China
7. Athens, Greece
8. Ireland
9. Tierra del Fuego
10. The Atlantic Ocean
11. Australia
12. Brazil
13. São Paulo, Brazil
14. The Continental Divide
15. Mount Denali (previously called Mount McKinley)
16. The Colorado River
17. The Colorado River
18. Tallahassee
19. The Apennine Mountains
20. The Alps

COMMODORE'S ADVANCED QUIZ #1

1. What is the only Middle Eastern country without a desert?

---

2. What lake forms the beginning of the Nile River?

---

3. In what Russian city would you find the Hermitage Museum?

---

4. What continent contains Queen Maud Land, Wilkes Land, and Marie Byrd Land?

---

5. What is the third largest state in the United States?

---

6. On what continent would you find the Atlas Mountains?

---

7. What African city is known as "the city of gold?"

---

8. In what country do the Tigris and Euphrates Rivers start?

---

9. What seas are named after colors?

COMMODORE'S ADVANCED QUIZ #1

10. What river flows through Prague, Czech Republic (Czechia)?

11. What is the largest city in Afghanistan?

12. What is Kentucky's nickname?

13. What is the most populated city in the U.S.?

14. What body of water separates Baja California from mainland Mexico?

15. Where is the Atatürk Dam Project located?

16. This country used to be known as Southwest Africa. What is its name today?

17. Among which four (4) islands is the Java Sea?

COMMODORE'S ADVANCED QUIZ #1

18. The most northern major island in this country is Hokkaido Island.

____

19. This group of islands is the farthest distance from any main landmass in the world.

____

20. These four countries are collectively known as Scandinavia.

____

ANSWERS TO COMMODORE'S ADVANCED QUIZ #1

1. Lebanon
2. Lake Victoria
3. St. Petersburg
4. Antarctica
5. California
6. Africa
7. Johannesburg (also known as Gauteng), South Africa
8. Turkey
9. The Black Sea, the White Sea, the Red Sea, and the Yellow Sea
10. The Vltava
11. Kabul
12. The Bluegrass State
13. New York City
14. The Gulf of California, also called the Sea of Cortez
15. Turkey
16. Namibia
17. Between Borneo, Java, Sumatra, and Sulawesi
18. Japan
19. The Hawaiian Islands
20. Norway, Sweden, Denmark, Finland

COMMODORE'S ADVANCED QUIZ #2

1. In what U.S. state would you find George Washington's home, Mount Vernon?

____

2. On which island is Pearl Harbor?

____

3. On what continent would you find Lake Titicaca?

____

4. What river flows through Lisbon, Portugal?

____

5. What state can you see if you look across the Mississippi River from St. Louis?

____

6. Where is the Henry Ford Museum located?

____

7. What river flows through London, England?

____

8. What country owns the Azores?

____

9. What U.S. state calls itself "The Beaver State?"

____

COMMODORE'S ADVANCED QUIZ #2

10. What river flows through Moscow, Russia?

____

11. What continent has the most people per square mile?

____

12. What U.S. city is at the junction of the Allegheny River and the Monongahela River?

____

13. What lake is the city of Sheboygan on?

____

14. What U.S. state is known as "The Last Frontier?"

____

15. Where do you go to row on the Po (River)?

____

16. Where is the Lut Desert?

____

17. What country covers an entire continent?

____

18. What body of water does the Colorado River empty into?

____

COMMODORE'S ADVANCED QUIZ #2

19. What is the largest freshwater lake in the world by volume?

----

20. What is the largest freshwater lake in the world by surface area?

ANSWERS TO COMMODORE'S ADVANCED QUIZ #2

1. Virginia
2. Oahu (a Hawaiian island)
3. South America
4. The Tagus
5. Illinois
6. Dearborn, Michigan
7. The Thames
8. Portugal
9. Oregon
10. Moskva River
11. Asia
12. Pittsburgh, Pennsylvania
13. Lake Michigan
14. Alaska
15. Italy
16. Iran
17. Australia
18. Gulf of California (also known as the Sea of Cortez)
19. Lake Baikal
20. Lake Superior

THE ADMIRAL'S ADVANCED QUIZ

The following cities and countries have changed their names.
Challenge yourself to fill in the blanks.

OLD NAME	NEW NAME	COUNTRY
1. Constantinople	_______________	______________
2. ______________	Burkina Faso	_______________
3. Lourenco Marques	_______________	_______________
4. ______________	Harare	_______________
5. Southern Rhodesia	_______________	_______________
6. Leningrad	_______________	_______________
7. ______________	Ho Chi Minh City	_______________
8. Peking	_______________	_______________
9. Alma-Ata	_______________	_______________
10. Gold Coast	_______________	_______________
11. Byelorussia	_______________	_______________
12. Northern Rhodesia	_______________	_______________
13. _____________	Tanzania	
14. _____________	Iran	
15. _____________	Russia	

THE ADMIRAL'S ADVANCED QUIZ

16. Someone who lives in China is called "Chinese." Someone who lives in Paris is called a "Parisian." What do you call someone who lives in Liverpool, England?

____

17. The aroma is so sweet and powerful throughout this valley that you can get dizzy from it. The name of this place is "The Valley of the Roses." What country is it situated in?

____

18. Liechtenstein is one of the smallest nations in Europe. Name three (3) others.

____

19. The name of this country means "beard."

____

20. Some places in the world are named after famous people. Name three (3) of them:

____

____

____

21. Which capital, by elevation, is the highest in the world?

____

22. Which continent has the most countries? ____________________

How many? ______________________________

THE ADMIRAL'S ADVANCED QUIZ

23. What language is spoken by more people than any other in the world?

____

24. Eight of the 10 tallest mountains in the world, as measured from Earth's surface, are in this country.

____

25. There are two countries in the world with the least amount of people per square mile of any country on Earth. Name one of them:

____

ANSWERS TO THE ADMIRAL'S ADVANCED QUIZ

1. Istanbul, Turkey
2. Upper Volta (or Haute Volta)
3. Maputo, Mozambique
4. Salisbury, Zimbabwe
5. Zimbabwe
6. St. Petersburg, Russia
7. Saigon, Vietnam
8. Beijing, China
9. Almaty, Kazakhstan
10. Ghana
11. Belarus
12. Zambia
13. Tanganyika
14. Persia
15. U.S.S.R. (Union of Soviet Socialist Republics)
16. Scouser
17. Bulgaria
18. Monaco, Vatican City (Holy See), San Marino, Andorra, Luxembourg
19. Barbados
20. Bolivia (Simon Bolivar); Ho Chi Minh City, Vietnam (Ho Chi Minh); Washington, D.C., and Washington state (George Washington); Lincoln, Nebraska (Abraham Lincoln); and San Francisco (St. Francis of Assisi).
21. La Paz, Bolivia
22. Africa – 54
23. Mandarin Chinese
24. Nepal
25. Mongolia or Namibia

THE EMPEROR'S SUPREME QUIZ

1. Bamako is home to over 2,600,000 people. In what country is it located?

---

2. The Alps is only one of several mountain ranges in Europe. Name five (5) others.

---

3. In the 1980s, a dictator named Nicolae Ceaușescu said, "Our capital is the only major city in Europe that is not on a river." He then enlisted more than 25,000 "volunteers" to divert the Dâmbovița River to his capital city. Name the capital city and the country.

---

4. In 2019, the capital of Astana was changed to this in honor of the country's longtime leader. What is its new name and in what country is it located?

---

5. What is the capital of the West African nation of Senegal?

---

6. What country is the most popular and most visited tourist destination in the world?

THE EMPEROR'S SUPREME QUIZ

7. The famous statute of the "Little Mermaid" is in this city ________________, which is the capital of ________________________________

8. Many people say that the best china is not made in China, but in Dresden. In what country is that?

____

9. Vladivostok means "Prince of the East." The name of that city has irritated the Chinese for years because that city is in a different country. What country?

____

10. This country has two official languages, English and French. From time to time the French-speaking part threatens to secede from the English speaking part. What is the name of the country?

____

11. The northern part of this country is so flat that some of its people have never seen a mountain, but you can go skiing in the "High Tatras," a mountain range in the extreme south. What is the name of this country?

____

12. This is the only country in Central America where teachers outnumber police.

____

THE EMPEROR'S SUPREME QUIZ

13. Name one of the most important rivers in Asia. It goes through parts of Vietnam, Laos, and Cambodia before it empties into the South China Sea.

____

14. These independent countries used to be combined to form the single country of Yugoslavia. What are they named today?

____

____

15. This island nation has the highest literacy rate per capita in the world.

____

16. The inhabitants of this country, the poorest in Europe, are called "Shqip" meaning "Sons of the Eagle."

____

17. Most rivers flow from north to south. Name two major rivers that flow from south to north.

____

18. Of all the continents, this one has the lowest maximum elevation:

____

19. Bird manure has made this country one of the wealthiest on Earth. (Yes, bird manure, also called "guano.")

____

THE EMPEROR'S SUPREME QUIZ

20-26: What were the "Seven Wonders of the Ancient World" and where were they located?

ANSWERS TO THE EMPEROR'S SUPREME QUIZ

1. Mali
2. Pyrenees, Jura, Carpathians, Apennines, Dolomites, Tatras, Balkans, Urals, Caucasus
3. Bucharest, Romania
4. Nur-Sultan, Kazakhstan
5. Dakar
6. France
7. Copenhagen, Denmark
8. Germany
9. Russia
10. Canada
11. Poland
12. Costa Rica
13. Mekong
14. Serbia, Croatia, Bosnia & Herzegovina, Montenegro, North Macedonia, Slovenia, Kosovo
15. Iceland
16. Albanian
17. Nile, Rhine, Elbe
18. Australia
19. Brunei
20. The Great Pyramid of Giza, Egypt
21. The Hanging Gardens of Babylon, Iraq
22. The Statue of Zeus at Olympia, Greece
23. The Temple of Artemis at Ephesus, Turkey
24. The Mausoleum at Halicarnassus, Turkey
25. The Lighthouse of Alexandria, Egypt
26. The Colossus of Rhodes, a Greek island near Turkey

YOUR FEEDBACK IS VERY IMPORTANT!

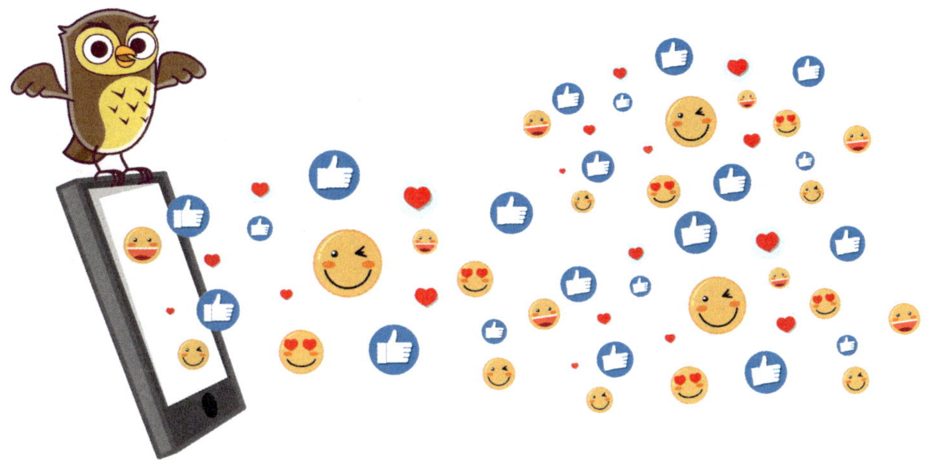

- If you enjoyed this book, visit our Facebook page at @OmniLearningCenter and share what you liked most about it, what you learned, etc.
- What type of guide would you like to see next? Write to Lorraine@OmniLearningCenter.org and let us know!

www.facebook.com/TheOmniLearningCenter

www.OmniLearningCenter.org

OMNI Learning Center Educational Guides

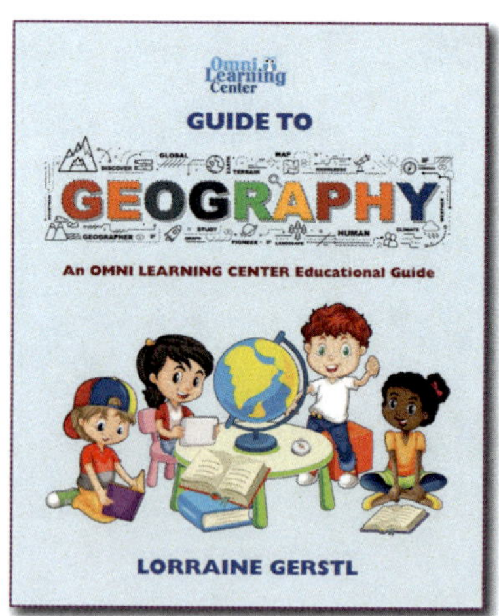

Made in the USA
Columbia, SC
23 December 2022

74889774R00088